HOW TO TELL A JOKE

ANCIENT WISDOM FOR MODERN READERS

■ ■ ■ ■

How to Tell a Joke: An Ancient Guide to the Art of Humor by Marcus Tullius Cicero

How to Keep an Open Mind: An Ancient Guide to Thinking Like a Skeptic by Sextus Empiricus

How to Be Content: An Ancient Poet's Guide for an Age of Excess by Horace

How to Give: An Ancient Guide to Giving and Receiving by Seneca

How to Drink: A Classical Guide to the Art of Imbibing by Vincent Obsopoeus

How to Be a Bad Emperor: An Ancient Guide to Truly Terrible Leaders by Suetonius

How to Be a Leader: An Ancient Guide to Wise Leadership by Plutarch

How to Think about God: An Ancient Guide for Believers and Nonbelievers by Marcus Tullius Cicero

How to Keep Your Cool: An Ancient Guide to Anger Management by Seneca

How to Think about War: An Ancient Guide to Foreign Policy by Thucydides

How to Be Free: An Ancient Guide to the Stoic Life by Epictetus

How to Be a Friend: An Ancient Guide to True Friendship by Marcus Tullius Cicero

How to Die: An Ancient Guide to the End of Life by Seneca

How to Win an Argument: An Ancient Guide to the Art of Persuasion by Marcus Tullius Cicero

How to Grow Old: Ancient Wisdom for the Second Half of Life by Marcus Tullius Cicero

How to Run a Country: An Ancient Guide for Modern Leaders by Marcus Tullius Cicero

How to Win an Election: An Ancient Guide for Modern Politicians by Quintus Tullius Cicero

HOW TO TELL
A JOKE

■ ■ ■ ■ ■

An Ancient Guide to the Art of Humor

Marcus Tullius Cicero

Selected, translated, and introduced
by Michael Fontaine

PRINCETON UNIVERSITY PRESS

PRINCETON AND OXFORD

Published by Princeton University Press
41 William Street, Princeton, New Jersey 08540
6 Oxford Street, Woodstock, Oxfordshire OX20 1TR

press.princeton.edu

Library of Congress Cataloging-in-Publication Data

Names: Cicero, Marcus Tullius, author. | Fontaine, Michael, editor,
translator, writer of supplementary textual content. | Cicero, Marcus
Tullius. De oratore. Liber 2.216–290. English (Fontaine) | Cicero, Marcus
Tullius. De oratore. Liber 2.216–290. Latin (Fontaine) | Quintilian.
Institutiones oratoriae. Liber 6. Caput 3. English (Fontaine) | Quintilian.
Institutiones oratoriae. Liber 6. Caput 3. Latin (Fontaine)
Title: How to tell a joke : an ancient guide to the art of humor / Marcus
Tullius Cicero ; selected, translated, and introduced by Michael Fontaine.
Other titles: Ancient wisdom for modern readers.
Description: Princeton ; Oxford : Princeton University Press, 2021. |
Series: Ancient wisdom for modern readers | Includes bibliographical
references. | In English translation with original Latin text;
introduction and epilogue in English.
Identifiers: LCCN 2020044600 (print) | LCCN 2020044601 (ebook) |
ISBN 9780691206165 (hardcover) | ISBN 9780691211077 (ebook)
Subjects: LCSH: Wit and humor—Early works to 1800. |
Joking—Early works to 1800.
Classification: LCC PA6308.D6 F66 2021 (print) |
LCC PA6308.D6 (ebook) | DDC 875/.01—dc23
LC record available at https://lccn.loc.gov/2020044600
LC ebook record available at https://lccn.loc.gov/2020044601

Editorial: Rob Tempio and Matt Rohal
Production Editorial: Sara Lerner
Text and Jacket Design: Pamela L. Schnitter
Production: Erin Suydam
Publicity: Jodi Price and Amy Stewart
Copyeditor: Jennifer Harris

Jacket Image: Cicero / Photo: Shutterstock, adapted by ajibson

This book has been composed in Stempel Garamond

Printed on acid-free paper. ∞

Printed in the United States of America

3 5 7 9 10 8 6 4 2

δοκεῖ δὲ καὶ γέλωτος οἰκεῖος ὁ Κικέρων γεγονέναι καὶ φιλοσκώπτης.

Cicero was seemingly addicted to laughter and to being a smartass.

—PLUTARCH,
*COMPARISON OF DEMOSTHENES
AND CICERO* (1.6)

CONTENTS

ACKNOWLEDGMENTS

Jocus est sapientia magna,
et jocus interdum plus gravitate valet.

A joke is great wisdom,
and a joke sometimes outwits severity.

— MATTHEW DELIUS,
THE ART OF JOKING (4.399–400)

Delius is right, so it is a pleasure to thank Rob Tempio for letting me play Perkeo in this series once more. I am also grateful to Valzhyna Mort, Mark Saltveit, Tessy Schlosser, and Joel Stein for sharing their insights on comedy or translation with me, and to the two referees whose excellent suggestions made everything better.

On a personal note, my heartfelt thanks go to Xiomara Gómez for her constant support,

and, of course, to Ava, Jake, and Alyssa. During the coronavirus lockdown of 2020, they were my first audience, and second, and third. . . . I thank them for humoring me.

Last, I would like to acknowledge the advice and encouragement of George Thomas, who writes under the name Quintus Curtius, with a proverb he will recognize:

> *Quam quisque norit artem, in hac se exerceat.*
> We each ought ply the trade that we know best.

Here I go.

ITHACA, NEW YORK

INTRODUCTION

Is humor a teachable skill, or is it something you're born with? A couple thousand years ago, Cicero had some thoughts about that.

Born in 106 BCE, Marcus Tullius Cicero made it to the very top of ancient Rome. Against all the odds, at the age of 43 Cicero found himself elected Consul—Rome's head of state, its chief executive, and commander-in-chief of its armed forces. He thwarted a coup attempt in his one year of office and was hailed as the savior of Rome.[1] When his term was up, he resumed his private practice as a trial lawyer, but he remained a power player in Roman politics ever after. In retirement, he wrote philosophical treatises of profound and enduring impact. And if *that*'s not enough, Cicero was

also, according to one ancient source, one of the two funniest men in history.

In the twilight of classical antiquity, a writer named Macrobius quoted many of Cicero's jokes in a literary dialogue called *The Saturnalia*. Centuries earlier, Cicero's secretary, Tiro, had made a collection of them. (That collection is lost today, but Macrobius and the other writers mentioned in this volume still had it.) And in introducing the jokes, Macrobius adds an arresting remark:

> The two most eloquent men that antiquity produced—the comedian Plautus and the orator Cicero—were also its two best at telling jokes. . . . Who doesn't know that Cicero's enemies routinely used to call him "the stand-up Consul"?[2]

That phrase, "stand-up Consul" (*consularis scurra*), is incredible. Cicero's opponents didn't

mean he was a solid guy. They meant he was a chief executive who behaved like a stand-up comedian.

Macrobius wrote five hundred years after Cicero's death, but he was echoing contemporary sources. Some of them are quoted by Cicero's biographer, the Greek essayist Plutarch (ca. 46–ca. 120 CE), who sized them up and said the same: "Cicero often got carried away with the ridicule and veered into stand-up comedy."[3]

Plutarch was getting at two things. One is an ambiguity inherent in all humor, the difference between laughing *with* someone and laughing *at* them. It can be a fine line, as a famous scene in American film illustrates.

HENRY (*laughing hard*). Really funny. You're really funny.
TOMMY. Waddya mean I'm funny?
HENRY. It's funny, y'know, the . . . the story. It's funny. You're a funny guy.

> TOMMY. Waddya mean? You mean the
> way I talk? What? [. . .] (*menacingly*)
> I'm funny how, I mean funny like I'm
> a clown? I amuse you? I make you
> laugh? I'm here to **** amuse you?
> Waddya mean "funny"? Funny how?
> How am I funny?
>
> — *GOODFELLAS* (1990)

The other thing Plutarch is getting at is the perilously fine line between a *stand-up comedian* and a *politician speaking in public*. Quintilian, the second author included in this volume, quotes an example of what Cicero's opponents had in mind (47):

> There was a candidate running for office
> whose father was believed to be a cook.
> When he went to ask a man for his vote,
> Cicero, who was standing by, piped up,
> "'Roast' assured—*I'll* support you!"

Frowning, Quintilian comments, "That's on the verge of stand-up (*paene scurrile*)."

Quintilian is right to be concerned. The line between wit and buffoonery can pose a serious threat to dignity. But it can also—as Cicero knew—be a source of power. As he emphasizes in his own discussion (244–247), *humor can collapse the distinction between an orator and a comedian*, between a political rally and stand-up comedy. Do it just right, and it'll bring you social and political power, even an election. It's a heady thought.

And right or wrong, jokes are the keys that unlock that power.

> A Roman soldier walks into a bar. He goes over to the bartender, holds up two fingers in a V, and says, "Five, please."

Great joke, isn't it? And yet it's the very kind Cicero and Quintilian were *not* interested in.

Rome did have a rich tradition of humor like that to draw on, from its Shakespeare-style stage comedies to its street performances and stand-up comedians. Yet Cicero and Quintilian turn their backs on it entirely. They are interested not in jokes as entertainment, but as weapons of war. The trial and the election are their battleground, and their soldier is the "orator," or professional public speaker. As Plutarch explains,

> Cicero would ignore protocol at trials and kid around, using irony to laugh away serious arguments. The point was to win.[4]

In the following pages, we will see many examples of what Plutarch means, for that is the primary feature, not a bug, of Cicero's technique. The art of winning the crowd (*conciliare*) through jokes is precisely the art that Cicero

purports to teach us. As a comedian wants to win the room, so the lawyer wants to win the case, and the politician, the election. A generation or two after Cicero, the Roman poet Horace captures why jokes are so effective at doing that:

> ridiculum acri
> fortius et melius magnas plerùmque secat res.

> A joke usually cuts through matters of
> importance
> more efficiently and effectively than
> severity.[5]

Solemnity is hard to establish but easy to compromise. A single wisecrack can expose the artificiality of serious proceedings—of a criminal trial, say—and change their course: *Ah, come on, man; how could we ever really know if that guy did it, or what actually happened that day?*

Isn't this all just a bunch of theater? And who are we *to judge, anyway?* A joke can do that. It can shatter the fourth wall as surely as a bullet shatters glass and send a jury's thoughts down that path. Telling one is a hugely risky strategy, but it just might pay off.

That said, like any weapons, jokes can backfire. People don't like being embarrassed in public and they don't forget it. Cicero considered himself a smartass. Others considered him a jackass, and reacted accordingly. Plutarch regarded Cicero's inability to resist a sick burn a causal factor in his downfall and eventual murder; that inability is a refrain in his *Life of Cicero*. The funny thing is, Cicero *himself* knew this. As he makes the narrator say in the treatise translated here,

And *that's* the hardest thing for quick-witted people to do: to take stock of the people, the circumstances, and to hold

back the quips that come to mind even when it would be totally hilarious to say them.[6]

> QUESTION. How do you tell the difference between a male chromosome and a female chromosome?
> ANSWER. Check their genes.

It's a funny thing, humor. In Latin, the word means *biochemical*. Today, we speak of chemicals, like serotonin and dopamine, and blame mood or misbehavior on chemical imbalances. Romans spoke of humors, like phlegm or black bile, and blamed mood and misbehavior on humoral imbalances. Funny how little some things change.

People in ancient Rome knew nothing of genes, of course, but plenty about genetics. They weren't stupid. They could see that some characteristics are acquired and others innate

(*innate* comes from their word for genetics, *natura*, meaning the condition of your birth). They could also see predispositions. It was obvious that certain abilities just come more easily to some people than others—sports, singing, public speaking, even telling a joke. In theory, if you were born with just the right balance of humors, like a Cicero, you'd be a humorous person. A wit. A natural.

What if you weren't, though? Could you become one? And if you *were* a natural, could you get even better? That question brings us to Cicero's treatise, the longest extant discussion of humor we have from the ancient world.

The Format

If you have a good idea to share with the world, there are a few different ways to present it. You can write an article or give a TED talk, or you can make it into a poem, or you can make it into a movie. The last option is the traditional for-

mat for humanistic learning. Instead of just telling us what to think—that's the easy option, and the one Quintilian chose—Cicero created a "dialogue" or script and constructed an imaginary world for readers to animate inside their heads. He creates real characters complete with individual personalities, and he distributes his thoughts on humor among them.

The treatise on humor presented here is self-contained, but Cicero embedded it in a much longer work called *On the Ideal Orator*. The work as a whole covers every aspect of the art of public speaking, and it is Cicero's masterpiece. Cicero wrote it in 55 BCE, eight years after his Consulship and twelve years before he was assassinated. But that's not when the dialogue is set.

Think for a moment. What was happening in your hometown 36 years ago? In ancient Rome in 55 BCE, that thought takes you back to 91 BCE. The Roman world is weeks away from

the awful and bloody conflict known as the Social War (91–87 BCE), and things are still quiet.[7] Cicero sets his dialogue there, and not in the capital city itself but in a villa in Tusculum, a nice suburb of Rome where the wealthy had their summer homes. He lifts the curtain on a number of famous orators of his grandfather's day discussing and reliving the glory days of their profession.

Ironically, the three speakers we meet in our extract are named Julius Caesar, Crassus, and Mark Antony, but none of them are the famous strongmen whose names will ring bells for students of Roman history. *This* Caesar is not the famous conqueror of Gaul but Gaius Julius Caesar Strabo Vopiscus (ca. 130–87 BCE), a famous wit of his time. Cicero singles him out elsewhere as *the* most hilarious orator in Roman history, and the other orators in the dialogue regard him as a pioneer of the light touch.[8] Glimmers of his wit sparkle here and there through-

out his speech (don't miss his pun in section 218). Five years after the dialogue takes place, he was assassinated. *This* Crassus is not the wealthiest man of the ancient world, but Lucius Licinius Crassus (140–91 BCE), one-time Consul and the greatest orator of his time. He died just days after the dialogue is set. And *this* Mark Antony is not the lover of Cleopatra but that man's grandfather, born in 143, Consul in 99, and, like Caesar Strabo, assassinated in 87 BCE.

Little need be said about Quintilian, the author of the second treatise included here. About ten years older than Plutarch, he was born around 35 CE on the far side of the Roman Empire, in Spain, and he devoted his career to the study of oratory. Like most professors, his life was remarkable only for his teaching appointments. Toward the end, when he held the first Chair of Latin Rhetoric in Rome, he wrote a master textbook on public speaking titled *The Education of the Orator.* As with Cicero's,

Quintilian's treatise on humor forms a separate module that he believes every orator should master. It will be immediately obvious that Quintilian had read Cicero's treatise closely, though his analysis of humor is different and interesting in its own right.

The Renaissance

With the fall of Rome in the West, Quintilian was to have the last written word on the theoretics of humor in Europe for 1,400 years. Both treatises were still studied in the Middle Ages, but it was only during the Renaissance that fresh ground was broken. The first original thinker to appear, Giovanni Pontano (1426–1503), finally coined an abstract Latin word for wit or humor, *facetudo*, and he goes on to explore its social virtues at great length.[9] Two generations later in Germany, the Protestant Reformer Philip Melanchthon (1497–1560) revisits

Cicero's and Quintilian's categorizations of jokes and emphasizes their tactical advantages, but with an updated framework taken from Aristotle and with new examples borrowed from biblical, ancient Greek, medieval German, and Protestant Christian history.

Melanchthon's essay appears as an introduction he wrote for the last serious humanistic treatise on humor, a didactic Latin poem titled *The Art of Joking*. The author was a young German named Matthew Delius (1523–1544). Delius died at the tragically young age of 21, leaving his poem in manuscript, and Melanchthon had it printed eleven years later. Unlike Cicero, Quintilian, and Melanchthon, however, Delius was not interested in the use of jokes as weapons or even in the old examples. As Barbara Bowen puts it (2003, 146), "For him, wit is essential, not to argument, but to recreation and friendly social intercourse."

Early on in Cicero's dialogue, Caesar half-seriously suggests that philosophers, not orators, are the ones to ask about where laughter comes from and how it works (section 235). In the nineteenth century, German philosophers, principally Schopenhauer, took up this cue with aplomb. Later came Freud and his alembicated explanations, which paved the way for psychology, psychoanalysis, and psychiatry each to take a crack at humor.

But that was a mistake. Jokes belong to rhetoric, not philosophy. As we're learning once again, asking a philosopher to analyze humor is a category mistake, like selling dolphin at a fish market.[10] And as we look back now, it seems Cicero knew it all along.

> QUESTION. Why is Spider-Man so good at comebacks?
> ANSWER. Because with great power comes great response ability.

INTRODUCTION

So, to return to Cicero's original question, *is* humor a teachable skill? Two millennia later, the jury's still out. No, says Jay Sankey. Yes, says Joel Stein. It's complicated, says Mark Saltveit. All three are comedians worth listening to.

Jay Sankey is a veteran stand-up comic and the author of *Zen and the Art of Stand-Up Comedy*. As he puts it,

> I do not believe someone can be taught to be funny. Not from a book, not from a thirty-two-week course. Either you're funny or you aren't. But if you are a naturally funny person, I believe you can learn to be a stand-up comic. . . . So though I don't believe "funny" can be taught, I do believe *stand-up can be taught to funny people.*[11]

Not so fast, says Joel Stein, a very successful comedy and sometime sitcom writer who wrote

Time magazine's humor column for 17 years. "Humor is math," he tells me, meaning it's reducible to a finite number of formulas and that yes, you can train yourself to do it. It's true, he says, that people's brains differ, and that some are more natural at it than others. But sitcom writers' rooms are proof that jokes can be worked out. Go look at one and you'll see: some categories even have their own labels, like "Hang a Lantern on It," and when you need a joke, you just reach for one.[12] This sounds suspiciously like the kind of categories that Cicero and Quintilian both end their treatises with. Yet Stein also tells me that some people *do* seem to need some baseline bent for humor.

The difference between these two views may be more apparent than real, Mark Saltveit tells me. Saltveit is a stand-up comedian, world champion palindromist, and philosopher of stand-up.[13] "There are two crucial distinctions," he says:

- The first is that stand-up comedy is an interaction between audience and performer in a particular moment in time.
- The second, and more important, is that Stein is describing comedic writing techniques, which obviously can be taught, whereas Sankey is referring to *a comic sensibility* as the thing that can't be taught. In other words, not *how* you make certain words funny, but what you *find* funny in the first place. Not the phrasing of your punch line, but your choice of subject matter, which often has more to do with social satire and the absurdity of modern life.

In this light, it's remarkable that Roman orators not only gave speeches but published them, too. Which audience were their jokes meant for? Perhaps it's time we ask the comedians about that.

A Note on the Translation

Styles of translation vary. Some are literal, others go for the gist. This one goes for the jest, and it can claim a good pedigree. "My job as translator," Cicero once remarked, "is not to be a bank teller, counting out coins for readers; it's to compensate them for the weight."[14] In that spirit, I've wracked my brains to find equivalent words, names, puns, phrasings, and cultural counterparts to make the jokes as funny in English as they are in Latin. I have also changed or suppressed details that would cause confusion or attract undue attention if kept in. You can call it paternalism, or you can call it good comedy. A comedian limits the distractions. So do I.

My style can also claim a long pedigree. The first person to translate Cicero's jokes was Plutarch, his biographer, around 100 CE. Two samples survive, and it is instructive to see how Plutarch handled them. The first is his version of the joke about the Sphinx that Quintilian

quotes in section 98, and it's literal (I quote it in the endnote). Since that joke is based on "the thing," Plutarch's approach makes sense. Not so the second joke, though, which is based on language.[15] Take a look:

> There was once a guy with an elite-sounding name. He looked like a Roman aristocrat, but rumor had it that he really came from North Africa (a place where, unlike Rome, most men got one ear pierced). When Cicero was speaking in court one day, the man called out, "I can't hear you!" Cicero replied,
>   "You sure *used* to have whole (hole-) doors in your ears . . . !"

"Certe solebas bene foratas habere aures."

Unlike me, Plutarch cannot replicate the pun on *bene foratas aures*, which means both *pierced ears* and *ears with fine doors in them*. So what

does he do? He reworks the punch line to honor its spirit. He chooses a word for *holes* (*trypētón*) that sounds like the word for *pierced* (*trētón*) and that suggests the holes or openings bored into a wind instrument:

> "And yet, you don't have your ear short on holes."
> "καὶ μὴν, οὐκ ἔχεις (εἶπε) τὸ οὖς ἀτρύπητον."

Is it (as) funny? Not to me, but Plutarch must have thought so. I follow in his footsteps here.

A Note on the Latin Text

My Latin texts are based on Kumaniecki 1969 for Cicero and Russell 2001 for Quintilian, though I have silently preferred a few trivial readings for Cicero found in the notes of Leeman, Pinkster, and Rabbie 1989 or May and Wisse 2001. I have freely changed capitalization,

punctuation, and spelling, and reformatted the text to highlight the punch lines. On Quintilian's own advice (*The Education of the Orator* 1.7), I have written *cum* when it means "with" but *quom* when that word means "when," "since," or "although," and I add long marks here and there to disambiguate forms. Inspired by Early Modern editions, I have also occasionally added diacritical marks to ambiguous adverbs and borrowed punctuation from Spanish to disambiguate the Latin. Last, I have added musical notes to both the Latin and the English to indicate the many quotations from ancient poetry, and subheadings to the English to articulate the structure of each treatise. With luck, it'll all be intuitive.

HOW TO TELL A JOKE

HOW TO TELL A JOKE

Cicero, *De Oratore*, Liber 2.216–290

ANTONIUS

[216b] . . . Suavis autem est et vehementer saepe utilis, iocus et facetiae; quae, etiam si alia omnia tradi arte possunt, naturae sunt propria certe, neque ullam artem desiderant.

In quibus tu longe aliis, meā sententiā, Caesar, excellis; quo magis mihi etiam aut (*1*) testis esse potes nullam esse artem salis, aut, (*2*) si qua est, eam tu potissimum nos docere.

HOW TO TELL A JOKE

Cicero, *On the Ideal Orator*, Book 2.216–290

"Humor Us, Caesar—Explain Jokes!"
Caesar Takes a Stab [216–234]

ANTONY

[216b] . . . Humor and joking, though, is fun and often wicked effective. Every other aspect [*of public speaking*] might be teachable by rules, but humor is obviously something you're born with and rules can't do anything for it.

Caesar, in my view you're far better than others at this, so you can easily back me up that joking either (*1*) isn't a teachable skill or (*2*), if it is, then you're the best person to teach it to us.

CAESAR

[217] Ego verò (*inquit*) omni de re facetius puto posse ab homine non inurbano quàm de ipsis facetiis disputari. Itaque, quom quosdam Graecos inscriptos libros esse vidissem "De Ridiculis," nonnullam in spem veneram posse me ex iis aliquid discere. Inveni autem ridicula et salsa multa Graecorum—nam ét Siculi in eo genere et Rhodii et Byzantii et, praeter ceteros, Attici excellunt—sed qui eius rei rationem quandam conati sunt artemque tradere, sic insulsi extiterunt ut nihil aliud eorum nisi ipsa insulsitas rideatur! [218] Quare, mihi quidem nullo modo videtur doctrinā ista res posse tradi.

Etenim quom duo genera sint facetiarum, alterum aequabiliter in omni sermone fusum, alterum peracutum et breve, illa a veteribus superior "cavillatio," haec altera "dicacitas"

CAESAR

[217] Actually, *I* think a decent funnyman can discuss *anything* with greater wit than wit itself. Let me explain. I once saw these Greek books titled *On Humor* and got excited, thinking I'd learn something from them. What I found, though, was lots of Greek quips and jokes—which makes sense, since the people of Sicily, Rhodes, Byzantium, and above all, Athens, are the leaders in this area.[16] But they were so ridiculous when they tried to schematize, systematize, and teach the "rules" behind them that the only thing I could laugh at was how ridiculous they were! [218] And that's why—to me at least—it seems impossible to teach a course in the topic you want.

The thing is, jokes actually come in *two* forms. The first kind permeate an entire speech, while the other come fast and razor-sharp. The ancients called the first kind "shtick" and the

nominata est. Leve nomen habet utraque res—
quippe! "Leve" enim est totum hoc risum
movere.

[219] Verumtamen, ut dicis, Antoni, multum
in causis persaepe lepore et facetiis profici vidi.
Sed quóm in illo genere perpetuae festivitatis ars
non desideretur—natura enim fingit homines
et creat imitatores et narratores facetos, adi-
uvante ét vultu et voce et ipso genere sermonis—
túm verò in hoc altero dicacitatis, ¿quid habet
ars loci, quom ante illud facete dictum emis-
sum haerere debeat quàm cogitari potuisse
videatur?

[220] ¿Quid enim hic meus frater [*sc. Catulus*] ab arte adiuvari potuit quom, a Philippo interrogatus quid latraret,

second "a sick burn." Both have funny names—
which makes sense, since the whole business of
making people laugh is (*winking*) "funny"
stuff.[17]

[219] That said, Antony, you're right. I've
often seen humor accomplish a great deal at
trial. But you don't need rules for that first category of ongoing banter [*i.e., shtick*], because
people are shaped by their genetics, and it's
that—plus some help from their facial expressions and voices and manner of speech itself—
which makes them funny impressionists or sto-
rytellers. And since that's true, then in the
second category [*i.e., sick burns*], too, where a
zinger has to get fired off and hit its target before anyone could seemingly even *think* of it—
well, how *could* there be rules?

[220] I mean, rules couldn't have helped my
brother Barker[18] here when Philip asked him,
"What are you howling for?" and he shot back,

"furem se videre"

respondit? Quid in omni oratione Crassus vel
apud centumviros contra Scaevolam vel contra
accusatorem Brutum, quom pro C. Planco diceret? Nam id quod tu mihi tribuis, Antoni,
Crasso est omnium sententiā concedendum.
Non enim fere quisquam reperietur praeter
hunc in utroque genere leporis excellens, ét illo
quod in perpetuitate sermonis ét hoc quod in
celeritate atque dicto est.

[221] Nam haec perpetua contra Scaevolam
Curiana defensio tota redundavit hilaritate
quadam et ioco; dicta illa brevia non habuit.
Parcebat enim adversarii dignitati, in quo ipse
conservabat suam;

quod est hominibus facetis et dicacibus difficillimum, habere hominum rationem et tem-
porum et ea quae occurrant, quom salsissime
dici possint, tenere. Itaque, nonnulli ridiculi ho-

"I see a thief!"

And what could rules have done for Crassus anywhere in that speech he gave in probate court against Scaevola or in the one defending Gaius Plancus against Brutus? Really, Antony, everyone thinks the honor you pay *me* should go to *Crassus*, because he's pretty much the only one you'll find who excels at both kinds of wit—that is, in the first category of keeping up the talk and in the second category of snappy comebacks.

[221] I mean, his entire *speech* defending Curius against Scaevola was bursting with goodnatured, category-1 ribbing. It didn't have those category-2 zingers because he wanted to spare his opponent's dignity—and in doing that, he kept his own.

And *that* is the hardest thing for quick-witted people to do: to take stock of the people, the circumstances, and to hold back the quips that come to mind even when it would be totally

mines hoc ipsum non insulse interpretantur
[222] dicere Ennium

♪flammam a sapienti facilius ore in
ardente opprimi quàm bona dicta
teneat;♫

haec scilicet "bona" dicta, quae salsa sint; nam
ea "dicta" appellantur proprio iam nomine.

Sed út in Scaevolā continuit ea Crassus atque
illo altero genere, in quo nulli aculei contume-
liarum inerant, causam illam disputationemque

hilarious to say them. Accordingly (and this is pretty funny), some jokers twist these [222] lines of Ennius—

♫"When his mouth's on fire, it's easier for a wise man to suppress the flames than a good remark (*bona dicta*)."♫

—to say:

♫"When his mouth's on fire, it's easier for a wiseass to suppress the flames than a good wisecrack (*bona dicta*)."♫

They claim the "good" or "helpful" part of Ennius's *dicta* obviously has to mean "funny" because *dicta* ("remark") already means "wisecrack" all by itself!

But as much as Crassus kept away from those in dealing with Scaevola and instead made light

lusit, síc in Bruto, quem oderat et quem dignum contumeliā iudicabat, utroque genere pugnavit. [223] ¡Quàm multa de balneis quas nuper ille vendiderat, ¡quàm multa de amisso patrimonio dixit! ¡Atque illa brevia!—quom ille diceret se sine causā sudare:

Minime mirum (*inquit*); modo enim existi de balneis.

Innumerabilia huiuscemodi fuerunt, sed non minus iucunda illa perpetua. Quom enim Brutus duo lectores excitasset et alteri "De colonia Narbonensi" Crassi orationem legendam dedisset, alteri "De lege Servilia" et quom contraria inter sese de re publicā capita contulisset, noster hic facetissime "Tres" patris Bruti "De iure civili libellos" tribus legendos dedit.

of the trial and their disagreement with the other kind—the one that doesn't entail roasting anyone—when it came to Marcus Brutus, who he hated and thought deserved abuse, he unloaded with both kinds. [223] He went *crazy* on the spa Brutus had recently sold off and the inheritance he'd burned through! And those zingers!—such as when Brutus said, "I don't see what I'm up here sweating for," and he snapped back,

"No surprise there: you *did* just get out of the spa. . . ."

There were *countless* ones like that, but the continuous banter was just as funny. I mean, Brutus called in a couple readers to quote from a pair of policy speeches Crassus had given to different audiences, and then pointed out sections where Crassus had allegedly flip-flopped. And *that*'s when our friend Crassus here asked

13

[224] Ex libro primo,

"Forte evenit ut in Privernati essemus ego
et M. filius. . . ."

Brute, testificatur pater se tibi Privernatem
fundum reliquisse.

Deinde, ex libro secundo,

(*cracking up*)—it was totally hilarious—*three* people to come read bits from the *three* books of the dialogue *On Civil Law* that Brutus's dad had written. Let me quote Crassus's rebuttal.

CAESAR QUOTES FROM CRASSUS'S REBUTTAL

[Caesar now quotes extracts from Crassus's rebuttal. The first three extracts begin with an inset quotation from Brutus's father's book, followed by Crassus's commentary.]

[224] First came book one:

> "My son Marcus and I once found ourselves at our villa in Privernum ..."

Brutus! Your father's going on record that he left you an estate in Privernum.

Then came book two:

"In Albano eramus ego et M. filius. . . ."

¡Sapiens videlicet homo cum primis nostrae civitatis norat hunc gurgitem! Metuebat ne, quom is nihil haberet, nihil esse ei relictum putaretur.

Tum, ex libro tertio, in quo finem scribendi fecit (tot enim, ut audivi Scaevolam dicere, sunt veri Bruti libri),

"In Tiburti forte adsedimus ego et M. filius. . . ."

Ubi sunt hi fundi, Brute, quos tibi pater publicis commentariis consignatos reliquit? Quod nisi puberem te, inquit, iam haberet, ¡quartum librum composuisset et se etiam

"My son Marcus and I were at our villa in Alba . . ."

This guy's *clearly* a genius, one of the smartest in the country! *He knew* (*glancing at Brutus*) this black hole. He was worried that once Brutus didn't *have* anything, people would assume he hadn't been *left* anything.

Then came book three, which is the last one he wrote (I heard Scaevola say there are three authentic books by Brutus):

"My son Marcus and I found ourselves holed up at our villa in Tivoli . . ."

Brutus, where *are* these estates your father left you? The bequest is recorded right here in this published treatise! If he didn't think you were already grown up, I guess your father would've written a fourth book to document that:

> "in balneis locutum cum filio"
>
> scriptum reliquisset!

[225] ¿Quis est, igitur, qui non fateatur hōc lepore atque his facetiis non minus refutatum esse Brutum quàm illis tragoediis quas egit īdem, quom casu in eādem causā funere efferretur anus Iunia? Pro di immortales, ¡quàe fuit illa, quànta vis! Quàm inexpectata! Quàm repentina! quom, coniectis oculis, gestu omni ei iminenti, summā gravitate et celeritate verborum, "Brute," inquit,

> "Quid sedes? Quid illam anum patri nuntiare vis tuo? ¿Quid illis omnibus, quorum imagines vides duci? Quid maioribus tuis? ¿Quid L. Bruto, qui hunc populum dominatu regio liberavit? Quid

"My son and I were having a conversation at our spa. . . ."

[225] Everyone, *everyone*, would agree that Brutus got brought down by this ribbing and those wisecracks just as effectively as by those "tragedies" Crassus acted out when, at the same trial, the funeral procession for a distant relative of Brutus's—an old woman—happened to come passing by. Good *gods*! You should have *seen* it, his zap! So sudden, so out of nowhere! Crassus fixed his eyes on Brutus, loomed over him with his every gesture, and, in a torrent of eloquence, intoned, "Brutus!":—

"Why are you just sitting there? What do you want that lady to go tell your father? What should she tell all those people whose funeral masks are parading by? What about your ancestors? What about Lucius Brutus, the man who freed this

te agere? ¿Cui rei, cui gloriae, cui virtuti studere? ¿Patrimonione augendo? At id non est nobilitatis. Sed fac esse, nihil superest; libidines totum dissipaverunt. [226] An iuri civili? Est paternum; sed dicet te, quom aedīs venderes, ne in rutis quidem et caesis solium tibi paternum recepisse. An rei militari? ¡Qui numquam castra vīderis! An eloquentiae? ¡Quae neque est in te, et, quicquid est vocis ac linguae, omne in istum turpissimum calumniae quaestum contulisti! Tu lucem aspicere audes? Tu hos intueri? Tu in foro, tu in Urbe, tu in civium esse conspectu? Tu illam mortuam, tu imagines ipsas non

nation from tyranny? What should she say you're doing with your life? What achievements, what accomplishments, what greatness should she say you're working on? Increasing the wealth you inherited? But real nobles don't do that, and even if they did—well, there's nothing left! You partied it all away! [226] Law school, like your father? C'mon. She'll tell 'em that when you sold the house, you sold your father's barrister chair right along with it! A military career? You've never seen a barracks! Excellence in public speaking? You're no good at it! Besides, you've used what tongue and voice you *do* have for that most shameful way of making a buck: badmouthing! Do you really have the nerve to appear in public, to look at these folks here, to show your face in the Forum, show it in Rome, show it to your fellow citizens? Don't you *panic* at the

21

perhorrescis? ¡Quibus non modo imitandis, sed ne collocandis quidem, tibi locum ullum reliquisti!"

[227] Sed haec tragica atque divina; faceta autem et urbana innumerabilia vel ex una contione meministis. Nec enim contentio maior umquam fuit, nec apud populum gravior oratio, quàm huius contra collegam in censurā nuper, neque lepore et festivitate conditior. Quare tibi, Antoni, utrumque adsentior: ét (1) multum facetias in dicendo prodesse saepe, ét (2) eas arte nullo modo posse tradi. Illud quidem admiror, te nobis in eo genere tribuisse tantum et non huius rei quoque palmam, ut ceterarum, Crasso detulisse.

> sight of that dead lady, at those masks
> going by? You've left yourself no *room*—
> not only to imitate them, but heck, even to
> *display* them!"

[227] It was a majestic performance, out of this world. His endless quips and zingers, though, you can remember from just a single speech of his, because there's *never* been such an epic display of prowess or public speech more impressive than the one he recently gave attacking his colleague in office, and never one so well-peppered with good humor. And that's why I agree with you, Antony, on both points: (*1*) jokes *are* often highly effective in public speaking, and (*2*) there's just no way to teach them systematically. I really am surprised you gave me so much credit in this area instead of awarding the crown to Crassus, as in every other area.

ANTONIUS

[228] *Tum Antonius* Ego verò ita fecissem (*in-quit*) nisi interdum in hoc Crasso paulum invi-derem. Nam esse quamvis facetum atque sal-sum, non nimis est per se ipsum invidendum; sed quom omnium sit venustissimus et urban-issimus, omnium gravissimum et severissimum ét esse ét videri, quod isti contigit uni, id mihi vix ferendum videbatur.

[229] *Hīc quom adrisisset ipse Crassus,*

Ac tamen (*inquit Antonius*) quom artem esse facetiarum, Iuli, negares, aperuisti quiddam quod praecipiendum videretur.

Haberi enim dixisti rationem oportere hom-inum, rei, temporis, ne quid iocus de gravitate decerperet; quod quidem inprimis a Crasso

ANTONY

[228] Actually, I would have, if I weren't a little jealous of Crassus about that. The thing is, there's nothing wrong with being a *very* funny person. But to be *the* wittiest, the *most* hilarious of all, and *at the same time* to be *and* to be acknowledged as the stateliest and most soaring of all—which applies to him alone—I really didn't think I could handle it.

[229] *Crassus grins, and Antony continues.*

Still, though, Caesar, when you claimed that joking is not a teachable skill, you put your finger on something that I *do* think needs to be taught.

You see, you said we need to take stock of the people, the case, and the circumstances, so that a joke won't compromise our authority—and it's true, Crassus really does do that. But this

observari solet. Sed hoc praeceptum *praeter-mittendarum* est facetiarum, quom iis nihil opus sit. Nos autem quomodo utamur quom opus sit, quaerimus, ut in adversarium et maxime, si eius stultitia poterit agitari, in testem stultum, cupidum, levem, si facile homines audituri videbuntur.

[230] Omnino probabiliora sunt quae lacessiti dicimus quàm quae priores; nam ét (*1*) ingenii celeritas maior est quae apparet in respondendo, ét (*2*) humanitatis est responsio. Videmur enim quieturi fuisse, nisi essemus lacessiti; ut in ipsā istā contione nihil fere dictum est ab hōc, quod quidem facetius dictum videretur, quod non provocatus responderit. Erat autem tanta in Domitio gravitas, tanta auctoritas, ut, quod esset ab eo obiectum, lepore magis elevandum quàm contentione frangendum videretur.

rule applies to *not* making jokes when there's no need of them. What we're *actually* interested in, though, is how to use them when we *do* need them, as for example against an opponent, and especially how to trigger a stupid, eager, light-weight witness when the audience looks receptive to him.

[230] In general, our comebacks are more impressive than our unprovoked cut-downs, for two reasons: (*1*) the quickness of a person's mind appears greater in a response, and (*2*) comebacks are indicative of good manners, since they suggest we never would've said anything if we hadn't been attacked. For example, in that very speech you mentioned [*in 227*], practically every quip Crassus made was a comeback to some attack. The colleague he was speaking against was such an authoritative, impressive figure that humor evidently stood a better chance of trivializing his allegations than arguments did of refuting them.

SULPICIUS

[231] *Tum Sulpicius* Quid igitur? ¿Patiemur (*inquit*) Caesarem, qui, quamquam Crasso facetias concedit, tamen multo in eo studio magis ipse elaborat, non explicare nobis totum genus hoc iocandi, quale sit et unde ducatur, praesertim quom tantam vim et utilitatem salis et urbanitatis esse fateatur?

CAESAR

Quid si (*inquit Iulius*) adsentior Antonio dicenti nullam esse artem salis?

[232] *Hīc quom Sulpicius reticuisset,*

SULPICIUS

[231] That's Caesar for you, folks: he concedes primacy in wisecracks to Crassus, though he spends a lot more time on them himself. So: should we let him off the hook, or should we make him explain this whole theory of joking to us, namely what it is and where it comes from, especially since he's admitting that humor is as powerful and effective as it is?

CAESAR

What if I agree with Antony that joking is not a teachable skill?

[232] *When Sulpicius has no answer to make, Crass chimes in:*

CRASSUS

¡Quasi verò (*inquit Crassus*) horum ipsorum, de quibus Antonius iam diu loquitur, ars ulla sit! Observatio quaedam est, ut ipse dixit, earum rerum quae in dicendo valent; quae si eloquentīs facere posset, ¿quis esset non eloquens? Quis enim haec non vel facile vel certe aliquo modo posset ediscere? Sed ego in his praeceptis hanc vim et hanc utilitatem esse arbitror, non ut ad reperiendum quid dicamus arte ducamur, sed ut ea, quae naturā, quae studio, quae exercitatione consequimur, aut recta esse confidamus aut prava intellegamus, quom quo referenda sint, didicerimus.

[233] Quare, Caesar, ego quoque hoc a te peto, ut, si tibi videtur, disputes de hoc toto iocandi genere quid sentias, ne qua forte dicendi

CRASSUS

Pfft! As if there were *any* "teachable skills" for all the subjects Antony's been talking about all this time. He said it himself: You can watch what works in public speaking, sure, but if that could make you an effective speaker, who *wouldn't* be an effective speaker?! Because, whether it came right away or took some time, who *couldn't* just learn to do that? My own view is that the power—the value—of these rules, is not that textbooks can help us figure out *what* to say; it's that once we've gotten something to say—from sheer inspiration, from thinking hard, from trying different things out—we can then either have the confidence that it's right, or understand that it's wrong, since we'll have learned a standard to check it against.

[233] And so, Caesar—if you'll do it—I too would like your thoughts on this whole theory of joking. That way (and this is what you all

pars, quoniam ita voluistis, in hoc tali coetu atque in tam accurato sermone praeterita esse videatur.

CAESAR

Ego verò (*inquit ille*) quoniam collectam a convivā, Crasse, exigis, non committam ut, si defugerim, tibi causam aliquam dem recusandi.

Quamquam, soleo saepe mirari eorum impudentiam qui agunt in scaenā gestum, inspectante Roscio. Quis enim sese commovere potest cuius ille vitia non videat? Sic ego nunc, Crasso audiente, primum loquar de facetiis et docebo sus, ut aiunt . . . oratorem—eum quem, quom Catulus nuper audisset, fenum alios (*aiebat*) ēsse oportere.

asked for), it won't look like we skipped over *any* aspect of public speaking in this fine gathering and exchange we're having.

CAESAR

Well, Crassus, since you're hitting up a guest (*indicating himself*) for a contribution to this party, I'll do my best. That way, if I *do* acquit myself, I'll give you no reason for refusing us *yours*!

I have to say, though, I'm always amazed at the chutzpah of actors who go on stage when a big star is in the audience. I mean, how can they do *anything* without him spotting their mistakes? That's me right now. With Crassus here listening, I'll be speaking about jokes for the first time. I'm going to be the proverbial "pig teaching the orator"—the *same* orator about whom, when Barker heard him speak the other day, he kept saying, "Put all the others out to pasture!"[19]

CRASSUS

[234] (*Tum ille*) Iocabatur (*inquit*) Catulus, praesertim quom ita dicat ipse, ut ambrosiā alendus
esse videatur. Verùm te, Caesar, audiamus, ut
Antoni "reliqua" videamus.

ANTONIUS

(*Et Antonius*) Perpauca mihi quidem restant (*inquit*); sed tamen, defessus iam labore atque iti-
nere disputationis meae, requiescam in Caesaris sermone, quasi in aliquo peropportuno
devorsorio.

CAESAR

Atqui (*inquit Iulius*) non nimis liberale "hospi-
tium" meum dices. Nam te in viam, simulac
perpaulum gustâris, extrudam et eiciam.

CRASSUS

[234] Barker was just kidding—especially since his own skills suggest *he's* been dining with the gods up in heaven. But let's hear you out, Caesar, so we can get to Antony's (*winking*) "feedback."

ANTONY

I really only have a couple things left to say, but I *am* pooped from all this talking—it's been a long trip. . . . (*Grinning*). I'll use Caesar's speech as a rest stop, like some perfectly placed motel restaurant.

CAESAR

Well (*grinning in return*), you're going to declare my "establishment" none too friendly, because as soon as you've had a snack, I'm putting you back out on the road!

[235] Ac ne diutius vos demorer, de omni isto genere quid sentiam, perbreviter exponam. De risu quinque sunt quae quaerantur:

(*1*) unum, quid sit;
(*2*) alterum, unde sit;
(*3*) tertium, sitne oratoris velle risum movere;
(*4*) quartum, quatenus;
(*5*) quintum, quae sint genera ridiculi.

Atque illud primum (*1*)—quid sit ipse risus, quo pacto concitetur, ubi sit, quomodo existat atque ita repente erumpat ut eum cupientes tenere nequeamus, et quomodo simul latera, os, genas, oculos, vultum occupet—¡viderit Democritus! Neque enim ad hunc sermonem hoc pertinet

The Caesarian Section [235–290]

Five Fundamental Questions

⌊235⌋ (*to everyone*) And so as not to keep you all waiting any longer, I'll outline the whole she-bang. When it comes to laughter, there are five questions to ask:

(*1*) What is it?
(*2*) Where does it come from?
(*3*) Should an orator want to make people laugh?
(*4*) If so, how much?
(*5*) What are the different types of jokes?

As for (*1*)—what laughter itself is, how it's aroused, where it dwells, how it arises and erupts so suddenly that we can't stop it even though we want to, and how it can simultaneously take over the sides, mouth, cheeks, eyes, and face—go ask Democritus for all that, because none of

et, si pertineret, nescire me tamen id non pu-
deret quod ne ipsi illi quidem scirent, qui
pollicerentur.

[236] (*2*) Locus autem et "regio" quasi
ridiculi—nam id proxime quaeritur—
turpitudine et deformitate quadam continetur.
Haec enim ridentur vel sola vel maxime, quae
notant et signant turpitudinem aliquam non
turpiter.

Est autem—ut ad illud tertium veniam—
(*3*) est plane oratoris movere risum,

(*3.a*) vel quod ipsa hilaritas benevolentiam
conciliat ei per quem excitata est,

(*3.b*) vel quod admirantur omnes acumen,
uno saepe in verbo positum, maxime respondentis, nonnumquam etiam
lacessentis,

it is relevant to what we're interested in, and even if it were, I'd have no trouble admitting I'm clueless, since even those who claim they do know, don't.[20]

[236] The boundaries of its home, though, the (*grinning*) "Laffin' Quarter"—which gets at question (*2*)—are formed by "disgraceful ugliness." I say that because the only thing that gets laughs, or the most anyway, are jokes that call out and stigmatize some disgrace in a graceful way.[21]

It's also—coming now to my (*3*)—it clearly *is* in the orator's interest to make people laugh, because:

(*3.a*) When you give people the giggles, they side with you reflexively; or

(*3.b*) Everyone admires a zinger—often (*winking*) "concentrated" in a single word[22]—especially in a comeback, though also as a first strike; or

(*3.c*) vel quod frangit adversarium, quod impedit, quod elevat, quod deterret, quod refutat,

(*3.d*) vel quod ipsum oratorem politum esse hominem significat, quod eruditum, quod urbanum, maximeque

(*3.e*) quod tristitiam ac severitatem mitigat et relaxat odiosasque res saepe, quas argumentis dilui non facile est, ioco risuque dissolvit.

[237] Quatenus autem sint ridicula tractanda oratori, perquam diligenter videndum est, (*4*) id quod in quarto loco quaerendi posueramus.

Nam nec insignis improbitas et scelere iuncta nec, rursus, miseria insignis agitata ridetur; facinerosos enim maiore quadam vi quàm ridiculi vulnerari volunt, miseros illudi nolunt, nisi

(*3.c*) It crushes an opponent: trips him up, ridicules him, deters him, defeats him; or

(*3.d*) It shows you that the orator himself is sophisticated, that he's educated, urbane; and most of all because

(*3.e*) It eases hurt and breaks the tension, and, when problematic facts can't be argued away, a joke and laugh often make them go poof.

Question 4: How Far Should an Orator Take It?

[237] How far an orator ought to take the laughs, though, is something to scrutinize with extreme care (this is the question I'd designated our [4]).

People don't laugh at making fun of obvious and criminal evil or, again, at obvious misery. People want *tough* vengeance on crooks, not jokes, and they don't like punching down on those less fortunate (unless, of course, those

se forte iactant. Parcendum autem maxime est caritati hominum, ne temere in eos dicas qui diliguntur. [238] Haec igitur adhibenda est primum in iocando moderatio. Itaque, ea facillime luduntur quae neque odio magno nec misericordiā maximā digna sunt. Quamobrem materies omnis ridiculorum est in iis vitiis quae sunt in vitā hominum neque carorum neque calamitosorum neque eorum qui ob facinus ad supplicium rapiendi videntur, eaque belle agitata ridentur.

[239] Est etiam deformitatis et corporis vitiorum satis bella materies ad iocandum; sed quaerimus idem quod in ceteris rebus maxime quaerendum est, quatenus. In quo, non modo illud praecipitur, NE QUID INSULSE, sed etiam si quid perridicule possis, vitandum est oratori utrumque, ne aut scurrilis iocus sit aut mimicus. Quae cuiusmodi sint, facilius iam intellegemus, quom ad ipsa ridiculorum genera venerimus.

people are virtue-signaling.). You have to be especially respectful of those held in high esteem, so you don't end up disparaging a darling of the people. ⌊238⌋ It's crucial to observe those restrictions when joking. They suggest that the softest targets are those that don't deserve deep hatred or extreme pity—hence, all the material that *is* available for jokes lies in the life problems of people who aren't highly respected, tragically afflicted, or fit for a hanging. Tease *those* problems cleverly, and people laugh.

[239] Disfigurements and physical flaws also offer pretty good material for jokes, though as elsewhere, we have to ask the crucial question of how far to take it. And the rule here isn't just THOU SHALT TELL NO UNFUNNY JOKE. It's that even if he *can* bring down the house, the orator has to avoid both kinds of joke, the stand-up and the street performer kind.[23] We'll get a better sense in a bit of what those are like when we come to the types of jokes themselves [*in 248*].

43

Duo sunt enim genera facetiarum, quorum alterum re tractatur, alterum dicto.

[240] (*4.a*) Re, siquando quid tamquam aliquā fabellā narratur; ut olim tu, Crasse, in Memmium,

"comedisse eum lacertum Largi,"

quom esset cum eo Tarracinae de amiculā rixatus. Salsa, ac tamen a te ipso ficta tota narratio; addidisti clausulam, totā Tarracinā tum omnibus in parietibus inscriptas fuisse litteras L L L M M. Quom quaereres id quid esset, senem tibi quendam oppidanum dixisse,

♫"Lacerat lacertum Largi mordax
Memmius."♫

The thing is, there are two types of humor. One depends on the thing (*res*), the other on the language (*dictum*).[24]

[240] (4.*a*) "On the thing" is any time something gets told like a little story, the way you once did to Memmius, Crassus. When he and another guy named Largus got into fisticuffs over a woman at a beach town, you said,

"He bit the guy's arm off and ate it!"

Funny, and yet you made it all up yourself! What's more, as a fillip you claimed the letters M M L L L were written on walls all over town, and that when you asked around, a local old-timer told you they meant:

♫"Memmius Mauled Largus's Limber Limb."♫

[241] Perspicitis genus hoc, quàm sit facetum, quàm elegans, quàm *oratorium*, sive habeas vere quod narrare possis (quod tamen est mendaci-unculis aspergendum), sive fingas. Est autem huius generis virtus, ut ita facta demonstres, ut mores eius de quo narres, ut sermo, ut vultūs omnes exprimantur, ut iis qui audiunt tum geri illa fierique videantur.

[242] (*4.b*) In re est item ridiculum quod ex quadam depravatā imitatione sumi solet; ut īdem Crassus,

"¡Per tuam nobilitatem, per vestram familiam!"

Quid aliud fuit in quo contio rideret, nisi illa vultūs et vocis imitatio?

[241] That's a perfect illustration for you of how *clever* this type is, how elegant, how perfect it is for public speaking, no matter whether you really have a real story to tell (though you might have to throw some fibs in), or whether you make it all up. And the beauty of this type is that you represent the facts in such a way that the character of the person you're talking about—his words, his facial expressions—they all come out so that the audience feels like it's all happening in real time.

[242] (*4.b*) Likewise, a "thing" joke is one that's based on parody. An example, once again from Crassus, is his

> (*melodramatically*) "In the *name* of your *nobility!* In the *name* of your *family!*"

What else was there for the audience to laugh at other than his face and voice imitations? And when he said

"¡Per tuas statuas!"

Verò quom dixit, et extento bracchio paulum
etiam de gestu addidit, vehementius risimus.

Ex hoc genere est illa Rosciana imitatio senis:

♫"Tibi ego, Antipho, has sĕro," inquit!
Senium est quom audio.♫

Atqui ita est totum hoc ipso genere ridiculum
ut *cautissime* tractandum sit; mimorum est
enim et ethologorum si nimia est imitatio, sicut
obscenitas. Orator surripiat oportet imitatio-
nem ut is qui audiet cogitet plura quàm videat;

"In the *name* of your *statues*!"

while stretching his arm out, and then adding a little waggle, we laughed even more hysterically.

A famous old-man impression from stage comedy belongs to this category (*Caesar imitates a young man imagining his father tsk-tsking at him*):

♫"It's for *you* I'm planting these trees, my son," he says!
(*in his own voice, muttering*) *That's* bitter old age when I hear it!♫

But precisely *because* this is all so intrinsically funny, you have to be really careful about it—since, as with obscenity, if you overdo it, you're in the territory of an impersonator, a caricaturist. The orator ought to sneak his impression in *subtly*, so that it leaves more to the audience's imagination than they see; similarly, he should

praestet īdem ingenuitatem et ruborem suum verborum turpitudine et rerum obscenitate vitandā.

[243] Ergo, haec duo genera sunt eius ridiculi quod in re positum est; quae sunt propria perpetuarum facetiarum, in quibus describuntur hominum mores et ita effinguntur ut aut re narratā aliquā quales sint intellegantur, aut imitatione breviter iniectā, in aliquo insigni ad irridendum vitio reperiantur.

[244] (*4.c*) In dicto autem ridiculum est id quod verbi aut sententiae quodam acumine movetur. Sed ut in illo superiore genere vel narrationis vel imitationis vitanda est mimorum et ethologorum similitudo, sic in hōc scurrilis oratori dicacitas magnopere fugienda est.

¿Quî igitur distinguemus a Crasso, a Catulo, a ceteris familiarem vestrum Granium, aut Vargullam amicum meum? Non mehercule in

put his good upbringing and decency on display by steering clear of foul language and obscene topics.

[243] Those two types, then, are the kind of humor that's based on the thing. They fall within the realm of shtick, which is where you describe and characterize people's conduct in such a way that telling a little story exposes the kind of person they are, or tossing in an impression reveals their involvement in some problem that's begging to be made fun of.

[244] (4.c) A joke based on *language*, by contrast, is one that's impelled by the "point" of a cute remark or idea. But just as in the last type—storytelling and doing impressions—it was incumbent on orators to avoid coming across as impersonators or caricaturists, so too, in this second type, they really have to shun the kind of wisecracks that belong in stand-up.

So how are we going to distinguish your friend Granius and mine, Vargulla, from Crassus,

mentem mihi quidem venit; sunt enim dicaces; Granio quidem nemo dicacior. Hoc opinor primum: ne, quotienscumque potuerit dictum dici, necesse habeamus dicere.

[245] Pusillus testis processit. "Licet" inquit "rogare?" Philippus. Tum quaesitor properans, "Modo breviter." Hīc ille: "Non accusabis—"

"Perpusillum rogabo."

Ridicule—sed sedebat iudex L. Aurifex, brevior ipse quàm testis etiam; omnis est risus in iudicem conversus; visum est totum scurrile ridiculum. Ergo haec, quae cadere possunt in quos nolis, quamvis sint bella, sunt tamen ipso genere scurrilia.

Barker, the rest? I for one have seriously never been able to figure that out. I mean, they're witty; *nobody* outwits Granius, at least. I suppose the first point comes to this, that it's not *necessary* for us to make a wisecrack every time it's *possible* to crack wise.

[245] A midget witness waddles up. "Mind if I ask you something?" says Philippus. "Keep it short," snaps the judge. "No problem," he replies,

"I just have a tiny bit to ask."

Boom!—Sitting in the jury box, though, was a member of the jury who was even *shorter* than the witness! All the laughter turned on him, and the joke came across as total stand-up. The point is that though wisecracks like these that can backfire and hit the wrong target *are* funny, they're still inherently like stand-up.

[246] Ut iste qui se vult dicacem—et, mehercule, est Appius!—sed nonnumquam in hoc vitium scurrile delabitur—: "Cenabo" inquit
"apud te . . ." huic lusco familiari meo C.
Sextio,

". . . uni enim locum esse video."

Est hoc scurrile, ét quod sine causā lacessivit ét
tamen id dixit quod in omnīs luscos conveni-
ret. Ea, quia meditata putantur esse, minus ridentur. Illud egregium Sexti, et ex tempore,

"Manūs lava (*inquit*) et cena."

[247] Temporis igitur ratio et ipsius dicacitatis
moderatio et temperantia et raritas dictorum
distinguent oratorem a scurrā, et quod nos cum

[246] Similar is your guy Appius, who wants to be witty—and, dammit, he *is*—but he sometimes slips into problematic stand-up. "I'll come have dinner at your house," he tells this one-eyed friend of mine, Gaius Sextius,

"I see you've got a place for one."

That's stand-up, not only because it was unprovoked but also because what he said would work for all one-eyed people. Those jokes don't get as many laughs because they look rehearsed. Sextius's comeback, though, was off the cuff and awesome:

"Go wash your hands and eat."[25]

[247] What will distinguish an orator from a stand-up comedian, then, is how each one takes the circumstances into consideration, how they moderate and temper their wisecracks, and how

causā dicimus, non ut ridiculi videamur sed ut
proficiamus aliquid, illi totum diem et sine
causā.

¿Quid enim est Vargulla adsecutus, quom
eum candidatus A. Sempronius cum M. suo fra-
tre complexus esset,

"Puer, abige muscas!"

—? Risum quaesivit, qui est meā sententiā
vel tenuissimus ingeni fructus. Tempus igitur
dicendi prudentiā et gravitate moderabimur;
quarum ¡utinam artem aliquam haberemus! Sed
domina natura est.

rarely they make them; and also the fact that *our* reason for making them is not to appear funny, but to achieve some objective; whereas *those* guys go on all day, and for no reason.

When a man was running for office, he and his brother went to give Vargulla a hug. Vargulla told his slave,

"Shoo these flies!"

I mean, what did Vargulla accomplish by saying that? He went for a laugh, which in my view is *the* flimsiest product of ingenuity. The lesson for us is, the time for wisecracks will be determined by long-term thinking and dignity—and I wish there were a *How To* manual for *those*! But genetics are in charge.

[248] (5) Nunc exponamus genera ipsa summa-
tim quae risum maxime moveant. Haec igitur
sit prima partitio: quod facete dicatur, id aliàs
in re habere, aliàs in verbo facetias; maxime
autem homines delectari, siquando risus con-
iuncte re verboque moveatur.

Sed hoc mementote, quoscumque locos at-
tingam unde ridicula ducantur, ex isdem locis
fere etiam gravīs sententias posse duci. Tantùm
interest, quod gravitas honestis in rebus et se-
veris, iocus in turpiculis et quasi deformibus
ponitur; velut isdem verbis ét laudare frugi ser-
vum possimus ét, si est nequam, iocari. Ridiculum est illud Neronianum vetus in furace
servo,

Question 5: What Are the Different Types of Jokes?

[248] (5) Let me now outline the types themselves that get the most laughs, starting with this first division: *Every funny remark sometimes gets its funniness from the thing and sometimes from language, but people love it when laughter is provoked by a combination of thing and language.*

Remember, though, that when it comes to observations, pretty much any observation I make and share for laughs can be used to make a serious point, too; the difference is that seriousness appeals to honor and important matters, while a joke appeals to slightly disgraceful, practically ugly ones.[26] For example, we could use the same words to praise a good slave or to ridicule him if he misbehaves. Nero's quip about a kleptomaniac slave is funny,

"solum esse, cui domi nihil sit nec obsig-
natum nec obclusum"

—quod idem in bono servo dici solet. Sed hoc
isdem etiam verbis; ex isdem autem locis omnia
nascuntur.

[249] Nam quod Sp. Carvilio graviter claudicanti ex vulnere ob rem publicam accepto et ob
eam causam verecundanti in publicum prodire
mater dixit—

"Quin prodis, mi Spuri? Quotienscumque
gradum facies, ¡totiens tibi tuarum virtu-
tum veniat in mentem!"

—praeclarum et grave est; quod Calvino Glaucia claudicanti—

"For him alone, nothing in our home is locked or sealed off."

—which is something we usually say about a good slave. This example actually uses exactly the same words, but in general, both funny and serious points are born of the same observations.

[249] For example, Spurius had an awful limp from an injury he got while fighting for his country. He was embarrassed to go out in public because of it, so his mother said to him,

"Why don't you go out, sweetie? With every step you take, you'll be reminded of your bravery!"

That's wonderful, serious; whereas when Calvinus was limping, Glaucia told him:

> "Ubi est vetus illud . . . ?—'Num claudi-
> cat?' At hīc, clodicat."

—hoc ridiculum est; et utrumque ex eo quod in claudicatione animadverti potuit, est ductum.

> "Quid hoc Naevio ignavius?"

severe Scipio; at in male olentem—

> "Video me a te 'chir'cumveniri."

—subridicule Philippus. At utrumque genus continet verbi ad litteram immutati similitudo.

"What's that old expression for checking in? '*Nothing hobbling, I hope?*' Well, here comes some hobblin'. . . ."[27]

That's funny—and yet both result from the fact that an observation could be made about limping!

"What greater knave is there than Naevius?"

Scipio asks that in earnest; whereas it got grins when Philippus told a smelly guy,

"It seems you've . . . (*sniffing*) . . . *goat* me surrounded!"

Yet, the similarity of two words—only one letter apart—is the basis of both the serious and the funny points.

[250] Ex ambiguo dicta vel argutissima putantur, sed non semper in ioco, saepe etiam
in gravitate versantur. Africano illi superiori
coronam sibi in convivio ad caput adcommo-
danti, quom ea saepius rumperetur, P. Licinius Varus—

"Noli mirari (*inquit*) si non convenit;
caput enim magnum est."

—laudabile et honestum. At ex eodem genere
est:

"Calvus satis est quod dicit parum."

Ne multa, nullum genus est ioci quo non ex
eodem severa et gravia sumantur.

[251] Atque hoc etiam animadvertendum est,
non esse omnia ridicula faceta. Quid enim potest tàm ridiculum quàm sannio est? Sed ore,

[250] People regard puns as the most ingenious of all, but they aren't always just jokes; they're often the basis of serious remarks, too. When Scipio Africanus kept trying to put a garland on his head at a party and it kept coming apart, Varus told him,

"Don't be surprised if it doesn't fit, for your head is great."

That was impressive and dignified. Still, this is in the same category:

"His name's 'Baldwin'?! Sounds right: he *did* win by a hair. . . ."[28]

In short, there isn't any type of joke that can't also be a source of serious and earnest remarks.

[251] And here's another point to take note of, that not everything people laugh at is witty. I mean, nothing makes people laugh quite like a

vultu, imitandis moribus, voce, denique corpore ridetur ipso. Salsum hunc possum dicere
atque ita, non ut eius modi oratorem esse velim,
sed ut mimum. Quare,

- primum genus hoc, quod risum vel
  maxime movet, non est nostrum: moro-
  sum, superstitiosum, suspiciosum,
  gloriosum, stultum; naturae ridentur
  ipsae; quas personas agitare solemus, non
  sustinere.

- [252] Alterum genus est in imitatione,
  admodum ridiculum, sed nobis tantùm
  licet furtim, si quando, et cursim; aliter,
  minime est liberale.
- Tertium, oris depravatio, non digna
  nobis;

clown: the face, expressions, the impressions he does, the voice, his whole entire *body* makes people laugh! So I *can* say he's "funny," but not the way I'd like an orator to be; he's funny like a street performer.[29] Hence,

- This first category—which maximizes laughs—isn't for us: too cynical, gullible, paranoid, virtue-signaling, stupid. Such people get laughs because they're walking stereotypes, and usually we give people like that a hard time, we don't act like them.
- [252] A second category consists of mimicry. It's really pretty funny, but we only get to do it on the sly, if ever, and in passing. Otherwise, it's not something gentlemen should do.
- Third is distorting the face. It's beneath us.

- quartum, obscenitas, non modo non foro digna sed vix convivio liberorum.

Detractis igitur tot rebus ex hoc oratorio loco, facetiae reliquae sunt quae aut (*1*) in re, ut ante divisi, positae videntur esse, aut (*2*) in verbo. Nam quod, quibuscumque verbis dixeris, facetum tamen est, re continetur; quod mutatis verbis salem amittit, in verbis habet leporem omnem.

[253] (*A.*) Ambigua sunt inprimis acuta (atque in verbo posita, non in re), sed non saepe magnum risum movent; magis ut "belle et litterate!" dicta laudantur; ut in illum Titium qui, quom studiose pilā luderet et idem signa sacra noctu frangere putaretur, gregalesque eum, quom in Campum

- A fourth, obscenity, is not only inappropriate to public life, but it should hardly be heard even at private parties.

So, once you rob public speaking of all these resources, the leftover humor resides in either (*1*) "the thing" (as I split it up earlier) or (*2*) the language. You see, when something's funny no matter what words you use for it, it's "thing" humor, and when something loses its zip if you change the language, it has all its fun in the language.

Jokes Based on Language (A.)

[253] (*A.*) Puns are supremely clever—they're in the "language," not "thing," category—but they often don't get big laughs so much as compliments ("Oh, *cute*, clever!"). For example, this soldier, Titius, liked to kick a soccer ball around at night and was suspected of breaking some important statues. When his friends asked why

non venisset, requirerent, excusavit Vespa Terentius quod

"eum bracchium fregisse"

diceret; ut illud Africani quod est apud
Lucilium:

♫"Quid Decius? Nuculam an confixum
vis facere?" inquit?♫

Ut tuus amicus, Crasse, Granius:

"non esse sextantis."

[254] Et, si quaeritis, is qui appellatur "dicax,"
hōc genere maxime excellit; sed risūs movent
alia maiores. Ambiguum per se ipsum probatur
id quidem, ut ante dixi, vél maxime; ingeniosi
enim videtur vim verbi in aliud atquè ceteri

HOW TO TELL A JOKE

he hadn't show up for his platoon's morning workout, Terentius Vespa quipped,

"Oh, it's okay—he said he broke an arm."

There's the one by Scipio Africanus, which Lucilius quotes:

♫"What about Decius? Want to make the kernel split?" he says.♫[30]

And Crassus, there's also the one by your friend Granius,

"Can't put on a price on it!"[31]

[254] And if you ask me, the kind of person we call a "smartass" best excels at this type of humor, but other types get bigger laughs. True, as I said before, a pun on its own is very highly esteemed, since the ability to change a word's

accipiant posse ducere, sed admirationem magis
quàm risum movet, nisi siquando incidit in
aliud quoque genus ridiculi. Quae genera, per-
curram equidem.

[255] (*A.1*) Sed scitis esse notissimum ridiculi
genus quom aliud expectamus, aliud dicitur.
Hīc, nobismet ipsis noster error risum movet.
Quod si admixtum etiam est ambiguum, fit sal-
sius; ut apud Novium videtur esse misericors
ille qui iudicatum duci videt. Percontatur ita:

[A.] Quanti addictus?
[B.] Mille nummûm.

Si addidisset tantummodo —

meaning to something other than what every-one else takes it to mean—that *looks* like the hallmark of ingenuity. Nevertheless, it results in admiration rather than laughter, unless it coincides with some other type of humor. I'll run through the various types.

[255] (*A.1*) You all know, of course, that the most familiar type of joke is where we're expecting one thing but something else gets said instead. In these cases, our own mistake makes us laugh, and if you stir in a pun, it adds zest. An example is the sympathetic seeming man in one of Novius's sketch comedies. The man sees this convicted debtor being taken away and asks him,

[A.] How much are you in for?
[B.] A thousand bucks.

If all he'd added was

[A.] Ducas licet!

—esset illud genus ridiculi praeter expectationem. Sed quia addidit—

[A.] Nihil addo, ducas licet!

—addito ambiguo, fuit (ut mihi quidem videtur) salsissimus.

Hoc tum est venustissimum quom in altercatione adripitur ab adversario verbum et ex eo, ut a Catulo in Philippum, in eum ipsum aliquid qui lacessivit infligitur. [256] Sed quom plura sint ambigui genera, de quibus est doctrina quaedam subtilior, attendere et aucupari verba oportebit; in quo, ut ea quae sunt frigidiora vitemus—est enim cavendum ne arcessitum dictum putetur—permulta tamen acute dicemus.

[A.] Sold!

then that would've been an example of a surprise joke. But because he added,

[A.] Not a denarius more!—Sold!

by adding a pun he became, in my view, totally hilarious.[32]

It's especially hilarious when, in a debate, one guy grabs a word from his opponent and flings it partway back at his attacker, the way Barker did to Philippus [*in section 220*]. [256] But since there are a whole lot of pun types and some heavy-handed theorizing about them, we really should be on the lookout for, and go looking for, good words. And even if we leave out the weaker ones as we do (because we have to make sure they don't come across as strained), we'll still wind up with tons of clever zingers.

(*A.2*) Alterum genus est quod habet parvam verbi immutationem, quod in litterā positum Graeci vocant "παρονομασίαν," ut:

"Nobiliorem mobiliorem."

Cato; aut ut īdem, quom cuidam dixisset, "Eamus deambulatum!" et ille, "Quid opus fuit 'de'?"

"Immo verò (*inquit*), quid opus fuit *te*?"

Aut eiusdem sponsio illa:

"Si tu ét adversus ét aversus impudicus es."

[257] (*A.3*) Etiam interpretatio nominis habet acumen, quom ad ridiculum convertas quamobrem

(*A.2*) There's a second type that involves changing a word slightly. When it's just one letter, the Greeks call it *paronomasia*. Examples include Cato's quip:

"Mr. Bickle? Pfft! Mr. Fickle."

And when Cato told a guy, "Shall we go for a walk, you and I? Yes, let's do!" and the guy asked, "Why do you need the 'do'?" Cato replied,

"Ha, no. Why'd I need the 'you'?"

And his famous wager,

"I'll betcha you're a queer who's into both the hanky *and* the panky."[33]

[257] (*A.3*) Interpreting names is also a clever jibe. That's where you make a joke out of why

ita quis vocetur; ut ego nuper:

"Nummium divisorem, út Neoptolemum
ad Troiam, síc illum in Campo Martio,
nomen invenisse."

Atque haec omnia verbo continentur.

(*A.4*) Saepe etiam versus facete interponitur,
vel ut est, vel paululum immutatus, aut aliqua
pars versūs; ut Stati a Scauro stomachante—ex
quo sunt nonnulli qui tuam legem "De civitate"
natam, Crasse, dicant—:

♫"St, tacete! Quid hoc clamoris? Quibus
nec mater nec pater est,

someone has their name. An example is my recent one about a political fixer named Cassius [*pronounced "Cash"-ius*]:

"Cassius and Youngblood both earned their names on battlefields: Youngblood got his at Troy; Cassius got *his* in the Campus Martius!"[34]

All these jokes are based on language.

(*A.4*) Often times, it's also witty to slip in a line of poetry, either verbatim or tweaked a bit, or part of one. An example is the verse from Caecilus Statius that Scaurus quoted to express his frustration (some say that moment was the genesis, Crassus, of your law cracking down on citizenship fraud):[35]

♫"Sh!!! Enough! What is with all this shouting? The *nerve* of you people

¿tanta confidentia?! Auferte istam enim
     superbiam."♫

Nam in Coelio sane etiam ad causam utile fuit
tuum illud, Antoni, quom ille a se pecuniam
profectam diceret testis et haberet filium deli-
catiorem, abeunte iam illo,

     ♫"Sentin' senem esse tactum triginta
          minis?"♫

[258] (A.5) In hoc genus coiciuntur etiam proverbia; ut illud Scipionis, quom Asellus omnīs
se provincias stipendia merentem peragrasse
gloriaretur:

     "Agas asellum," etc.

who have no mother or father! Knock off
the arrogance!"♫

And Antony, that quote you worked in really
helped you neutralize Coelius in your [*bribery*]
case when he testified that yes, he'd authorized
the release of some money [*to pay the bribe*]. He
had a son who was a bit of a metrosexual, so as
he was leaving the witness stand, you quipped,

♫"You see? The old man's been bilked of
thirty bucks!"[36]♫

[258] (*A.5*) Proverbs belong to this category, too.
A famous example is when Burrows was brag-
ging that in the course of his military service,
he'd visited every province. Scipio quipped:

"You have to *drive* a burro, it won't be
taught the way."

Quare, ea quoque—quoniam mutatis verbis non possunt retinere eandem venustatem—non in re, sed in verbis posita ducantur.

[259] (*A.6*) Est etiam in verbo positum non insulsum genus ex eo, quom ad verbum, non ad sententiam, rem accipere videare; ex quo uno genere totus est *Tutor*, mimus vetus, oppido ridiculus. Sed abeo a mimis; tantùm huius genus ridiculi insigni aliquā et notā re notari volo.

Est autem ex hōc genere illud quod tu, Crasse, nuper ei qui te rogasset num tibi molestus esset futurus si ad te, bene ante lucem, venisset:

[A.] Tu verò (*inquisti*) molestus non eris.
[B.] Iubebis igitur te (*inquit*) suscitari?
[A.] *Et tu*:

And that's why—because they lose their magic if you change the words—they too should be classified not as "thing" but as "language" humor.

[259] (*A.6*) There's another category of language-based humor, too—and a good one—when you seem to take something literally instead of the way it's meant. The old street-performance skit *The Babysitter* is entirely based on this idea, and it's freaking hilarious. But forget skits—I just wanted a famous illustration to illustrate this category of humor.

This is, though, the category to which that quip of yours belongs, Crassus. A guy recently asked if he'd be bothering you if he came over really early in the morning.

[A.] "No, you won't bother me," you told him.
[B.] "So you'll set an alarm?" he asked.
[A.] And you went,

"Certe negaram te molestum futurum."

[260] Ex eodem hoc, vetus illud est quod aiunt Maluginensem illum Scipionem, quom ex centuriā suā renuntiaret Acidinum consulem praecoque dixisset, "Dic de L. Manlio":

"Virum bonum (*inquit*) egregiumque civem esse arbitror."

Ridicule illud etiam L. Nasica censori Catoni, quom ille: "Ex tui animi sententiā tu uxorem habes?"

"Non hercule (*inquit*) ex mei animi sententiā."

"As I said, you definitely won't be bothering me."[37]

[260] Of this same sort is the quip attributed to Scipio Maluginensis, in announcing that his bloc was voting as one for (Lucius Manlius) Acidinus as Consul. When the electoral official posed the formal question [*of a different candidate*], "What say you of Lucius Manlius?" Scipio replied,

"In my view, he is a gentleman and a patriot."

Another good one is what a man told Cato when he was updating the census lists. When Cato asked him the formulaic question, "Upon your oath, do you warrant you have a wife?" "Lord, yes!" he quipped,

"And emphasis on 'war'!"[38]

Haec aut frigida sunt, aut tum salsa quom aliud est expectatum. Naturā enim nos, ut ante dixi, noster delectat error; ex quo, quom quasi decepti sumus expectatione, ridemus.

[261] In verbis etiam illa sunt quae aut

(*A.7*) ex immutatā oratione ducuntur, aut
(*A.8*) ex unius verbi translatione, aut
(*A.9*) ex inversione verborum.

(*A.7*) Ex immutatione, ut olim Rusca quom legem ferret annalem, dissuasor M. Servilius, "Dic mihi" (*inquit*) "M. Pinari, num, si contra te dixero, ¿mihi male dicturus es, ut ceteris fecisti?":

"Ut sementem feceris, ita metes" (*inquit*).

These jokes are weak, or else they're funny when they surprise us, because, as I said before [*in section 255*], our mistake naturally delights us, so that when our expectations fool us (as it were), we laugh.

[261] Other types of "language" humor are those that come from

(*A.7*) adapting an utterance to the circumstances, or
(*A.8*) twisting a word, or
(*A.9*) verbal jujitsu.

An example of (*A.7*) is when Rusca was once proposing a minimum-age-to-hold-office law. Servilius opposed it, and asked, "Tell me, Rusca: if I speak against you, are you going to abuse me the way you did all the others?" Rusca replied,

"As you sow, so you shall reap."[39]

[262] (*A.8*) Ex translatione autem, ut quom Scipio ille maior, Corinthiis statuam pollicentibus eo loco ubi aliorum essent imperatorum,

"turmalīs (*dixit*) displicere."

(*A.9*) Invertuntur autem verba, ut Crassus apud M. Perpernam iudicem pro Aculeone quom diceret, aderat contra Aculeonem Gratidiano L. Aelius Lamia, deformis, ut nostis; qui quom interpellaret odiose,

"Audiamus (*inquit*) pulchellum puerum" (*Crassus*).

Quom esset adrisum, "Non potui mihi," inquit Lamia, "formam ipse fingere, ingenium potui." Tum hic,

[262] An example of (*A.8*), though, is when the people of Corinth were promising the famous Scipio the Elder a statue in the same area as all their other generals'. He quipped,

"I'm not a 'company' guy."[40]

As for (*A.9*), verbal jujitsu: When Crassus was speaking on behalf of Aculeo before Marcus Perpena, presiding, a witness for the opposing counsel was Lucius Aelius Lamia—pug ugly, as you know. When he kept interrupting and being a pain in the ass, Crassus quipped,

"Alright, let's hear from this cute little thang."

When everyone snickered, Lamia replied, "I had no say-so in my appearance, but I did with my mind." So Crassus quipped,

"Audiamus (*inquit*) disertum."

Multo etiam adrisum est vehementius.

(*A. 10*) Sunt etiam illa venusta, út in gravibus sententiis, síc in facetiis (dixi enim dudum materiam esse aliam ioci, aliam severitatis; generum autem et locorum, unam esse rationem). [263] Ornant igitur inprimis orationem verba relata contrarie; quod idem genus est saepe etiam facetum; ut Servius ille Galba, quom iudices L. Scribonio tribuno plebis ferret familiarīs suos et dixisset Libo, "Quando tandem, Galba, de triclinio tuo exibis?"

"Quom tu (*inquit*) de cubiculo alieno."

"Alright, let's hear from this genius."

People cracked up laughing even harder.

(*A.10*) These next ones are also great for both serious points and wisecracks (because remember, as I said a while ago [*in sections 248–250*], the *material* for a joke is different from that of a serious statement, but the system of their categories and the observations they rely on are the same). [263] So, a proven trick for dressing up a public address is to make words face off against each other, and that category's often witty, too. For example, Libo was in charge of a jury selection. When Galba kept proposing his own friends, Libo asked, "Jeez, Galba, when *will* you get out of your living room?" He replied,

"As soon as you get out of other people's bedrooms."

A quo genere ne illud quidem plurimum distat
quod Glaucia Metello:

"Villam in Tiburti habes, cohortem in
Palatio."

[264] Ac (*A.*) verborum quidem genera quae essent faceta, dixisse me puto; (*B.*) rerum plura
sunt, eaque magis, ut dixi ante, ridentur.

(*B.1*) In quibus est narratio, res sane difficilis.
Exprimenda enim sunt et ponenda ante oculos
ea quae videantur ét verisimilia (quod est proprium narrationis) ét quae sint (quod ridiculi
proprium est) subturpia; cuius exemplum, ut
brevis sim, sit sane illud quod ante posui Crassi

Not much different from this type is Glaucia's quip to Metellus [*about the many hangers-on thronging his fancy townhouse in Rome's trendiest neighborhood*]:

"You have a farm out in Tivoli, but all your pigs here on the Palatine!"

[264] And with that, I think I've covered all the (*A.*) types of humor that depend on language. There are a greater number that (*B.*) depend on things, though, and as I said earlier, they get more laughs.

Jokes Based on Things (B.)

(*B.1*) One of them is telling a story, which is really pretty hard, because you have to say and get people to imagine things that seem both plausible (which is a requirement of a story) and a little politically incorrect (which is a requirement of humor). As a quick example of what I

de Memmio. Et ad hoc genus adscribamus etiam narrationes apologorum.

[265] (*B.2*) Trahitur etiam aliquid ex historiā; ut quom Sex. Titius se "Cassandram" esse diceret,

"Multos (*inquit Antonius*) possum tuos Aiaces Oileos nominare."

Est etiam ex similitudine, quae aut collationem habet aut tamquam imaginem collationis; ut ille Gallus olim testis in Pisonem, quom innumera-bilem Magio praefecto pecuniam dixisset datam idque Scaurus tenuitate Magi redargueret,

mean, take Crassus's one about Memmius that I told before [*in section 240*]. Oh, and let's add Aesop's fables and the like to this category.

⌊265⌋ (*B.2*) You also get some good stuff from history, such as when Sextus Titius kept calling himself Cassandra. Antony quipped,

"I can name names of many of your Oily Ajaxes."[41]

The same goes for likeness, which involves a comparison or the "ghost" of a comparison. For example, on one occasion a man was testifying against Piso [*on a charge of extorting the natives*]. He claimed Piso's colonial officer, Magius, had been given a gigantic sum of money. When Scaurus rebutted the claim by pointing to Magius's poverty, the man replied, "Wrong, Scaurus—I never said Magius saved the money."

"Erras (*inquit*), Scaure; ego enim Magium non 'conservasse' dico, sed, tamquam nudus nuces legeret, 'in ventre abstulisse.'"

Ut illud M. Cicero senex, huius viri optimi nostri familiaris pater:

"Nostros homines similes esse Syrorum venalium: út quisque optime Graece sciret, íta esse nequissimum."

[266] Valde autem ridentur etiam imagines, quae fere in deformitatem aut in aliquod vitium corporis ducuntur, cum similitudine turpioris; ut meum illud in Helvium Manciam: "Iam ostendam cuius modi sis." Quom ille, "Ostende, quaeso," demonstravi digito pictum Gallum in Mariano scuto Cimbrico, sub Novis, distortum,

"I'm saying he's like the man with no clothes collecting peanuts: he squirreled it away in his belly."

Another is the remark that Marcus Cicero senior, the father of our fine fellow here,[42] came up with:

"Our Romans are like Middle Eastern slaves for sale: the better they know Greek, the less you want them."

[266] Portraits also get big laughs. They latch on to some physical flaw or problem and compare it to something even worse. An example is my swipe at Helvius Mancia. "Now I'm going to show you what you're like," I say. "Be my guest," he says. Now, one of the shields Marius captured in the Cimbric War was hanging near the New Shops [*in the Forum*]. So I pointed at

eiectā linguā, buccis fluentibus. Risus est commotus; nihil tam Manciae simile visum est.

Ut quom testi Pinario mentum in dicendo intorquenti,

"Tum ut diceret, si quid vellet, si nucem fregisset."

[267] (*B.3*) Etiam illa, quae minuendi aut augendi causā ad incredibilem admirationem efferuntur; velut tu, Crasse, in contione,

"Ita sibi ipsum magnum videri Memmium ut in Forum descendens, caput ad fornicem Fabianum demitteret."

the Gaul depicted on it, who was grimacing with bulging cheeks and had his tongue sticking out. Laughter erupted because it looked exactly like Mancia.

Another one is when Pinarius was on the witness stand and kept shifting his jaw as he spoke. I told him,

> "Please go on, if you like—as soon as you're done cracking that walnut."

[267] (*B.3*) There are also those statements that, in order to underplay or exaggerate something, surprise us by going totally over the top. For instance, in one public speech, Crassus, you quipped:

> "Memmius thinks he's such a towering figure that when he comes into the Forum, he has to duck under the Fabian arch."

Ex quo genere etiam illud est quod Scipio apud Numantiam, quom stomacharetur cum C. Metello, dixisse dicitur,

> "Si quintum parĕret mater eius, asinum fuisse parituram."

[268] (*B.4*) Arguta etiam significatio est, quom parvā re (et saepe, verbo) res obscura et latens illustratur; ut quom C. Fabricio P. Cornelius homo, ut existimabatur, avarus et furax, sed egregie fortis et bonus imperator, gratias ageret quod se homo inimicus consulem fecisset, bello praesertim magno et gravi:

> "Nihil est quod mihi gratias agas (*inquit*), si malui compilari quàm vēnire."

Another example in this category is Scipio's quip in Numantia. They say he was so angry at a [*stupid*] guy that he said,

> "If his mother had had one more kid, it would've been a donkey!"

[268] (*B.4*) Also witty is intimation, where a detail—sometimes just a word—brings to light something latent or left unsaid. For example, Cornelius was a man known for greed and corruption, but also as an exceptionally brave and capable general in the army. He went to thank Fabricius for voting for him as Consul, even though they were enemies and in the middle of a long and difficult war. "No need to thank me," Fabricius quipped.

> "Better to be robbed than sold" [*into slavery, as soldiers defeated in war routinely were*].

Ut Asello Africanus, obicienti lustrum illud
infelix:

"Noli (*inquit*) mirari; is enim qui te ex
aerariis exemit, lustrum condidit et tau-
rum immolavit."

[269] (*B.5.a*) Urbana etiam dissimulatio est,
quom alia dicuntur àc sentias—non illo genere
(de quo ante dixi) quom contraria dicas, ut La-
miae Crassus—sed quom toto genere orationis
severe ludas, quom aliter sentias àc loquare; ut
noster Scaevola Septumuleio illi Anagnino, cui
pro C. Gracchi capite erat aurum repensum,

Here's another example. When Burrows blamed a notorious half-decade of bad harvests [*during Scipio Africanus's term in office as Censor*] on Scipio, Scipio told him,

> "What'd you expect? I mean, the man who finished the census and sought the gods' blessing is the same one who saved *your* sorry ass from demotion."[43]

[269] (*B.5.a*) Also sophisticated is feigning ignorance, which is where you say something different from what you think. I don't mean the kind I talked about earlier, where you say the opposite, like Crassus did to Lamia [*in section 262*]. I mean where you're being mock-serious with every aspect of your speaking, all while thinking something different from what you're saying. An example is our friend Scaevola. In exchange for the head of Gaius Gracchus, a man named Septumuleius had been paid

roganti ut se in Asiam praefectum duceret,

"Quid tibi vis (*inquit*), insane? Tanta malorum civium est multitudo ut tibi ego hoc confirmem: si Romae manseris, paucis annis te ad maximas pecunias esse venturum."

[270] Hōc in genere Fannius in Annalibus suis Africanum hunc Aemilianum dicit fuisse et eum Graeco verbo appellat "εἴρωνα"; sed uti ei ferunt qui melius haec norunt, Socraten opinor in hac εἰρωνείᾳ dissimulantiāque longe lepore et humanitate omnibus praestitisse. Genus est perelegans et cum gravitate salsum, cúmque oratoriis dictionibus túm urbanis sermonibus accommodatum.

[271] (Et hercule omnia haec quae a me de facetiis disputantur, non maiora forensium ac-

its weight in gold. When Septumuleius subsequently asked Scaevola to bring him on to Asia Minor as one of his colonial officers, Scaevola said,

"What are you, nuts? Trust me, we have so many bad citizens right here in Rome that if you just stay put, in a few years you'll be rich beyond belief."

[270] In his *Annals*, Fannius says Scipio Aemilianus adopted this mode and calls him "ironic," using that Greek word. But like the experts, when it comes to this "irony" and feigned ignorance, I think Socrates far outdid everyone in both charm and kindness. It's a very elegant type of humor, both funny and serious at the same time. It's suitable both for public speaking and for conversational banter.

[271] (To be honest, *all* these points I've been making about humor are salsa that's just as good

tionum quàm omnium sermonum condimenta sunt. Nam sícut quod apud Catonem est—qui multa rettulit, ex quibus a me exempli causā complura ponuntur—per- mihi -scitum videtur, C. Publicium solitum esse dicere, "P. Mummium cuiusvis temporis hominem esse," síc profecto se res habet, nullum ut sit vitae tempus in quo non deceat leporem humanitatemque versari. Sed redeo ad cetera.)

[272] (*B.5.b*) Est huic finitimum dissimulationi, quom honesto verbo vitiosa res appellatur; ut, quom Africanus censor tribu movebat eum centurionem qui in Pauli pugnā non adfuerat, quom ille se custodiae causa diceret in castris remansisse quaereretque cur ab eo notaretur,

on conversation of any kind as on trials. For example, one that's in a book by Cato [*the Elder*]—he collected a bunch of them, and it's where I've been getting quite a few of my examples—seems exceptionally clever to me. Gaius Publicius used to say that Publius Mummius was a "good at any time" guy. And dammit, it really *is* the case that there's no time of life when charm and kindness shouldn't be involved. But let me get back to the rest of my points.)

[272] (*B.5.b*) Bordering on the feigned ignorance that I've been talking about is calling a flawed thing by a good name. For example, when Scipio Africanus was Censor, he expelled from his tribe a centurion who had not been present at the Battle of Pydna. When the man claimed he'd stayed back at the camp to guard it and asked why he was being punished for that, Scipio answered,

"Non amo (*inquit*) nimium diligentīs."

[273] (*B.5.c*) Acutum etiam illud est, quom ex alterius oratione aliud excipias atquè ille vult; ut Salinatori Maximus, quom Tarento amisso arcem tamen Livius retinuisset multaque ex eā proelia praeclara fecisset, quom aliquot post annis Maximus id oppidum recepisset rogaretque eum Salinator ut meminisset operā suā se Tarentum recepisse, "Quidni (*inquit*) meminerim?

"Numquam enim recepissem, nisi tu perdidisses."

[274] (*B.5.d*) Sunt etiam illa subabsurda, sed eo ipso nomine saepe ridicula, non solum mimis

"I don't like people who are too diligent."

[273] (*B.5.c*) Also funny is when you take something another person says differently from the way it was meant. An example is what Fabius Maximus told Livius Salinator. We'd lost Tarentum, but Livius had still managed to hold on to its citadel, and he then used it as a base for launching a number of glorious battles. Some years later Maximus took the town back, and Salinator asked him, "Will you remember that it's thanks to *my* efforts that you took Tarentum back?" "Forget? How could I?" Maximus asked.

"I never could've taken it back if you hadn't lost it."

[274] (*B.5.d*) There are also non sequiturs, which are often funny for that very reason. They're

perapposita, sed etiam quodam modo nobis:

"Homo fatuus, postquam rem habere coepit, est emortuus."

[A.] "Quid est tibi ista mulier?"
[B.] "Uxor."
[A.] "Similis, medius fidius!"

"Quamdiu ad aquas fuit, numquam est
emortuus."

Genus hoc levius et (ut dixi) mimicum, sed
habet nonnumquam aliquid etiam apud nos
loci; ut vel non stultus quasi stulte cum sale
dicat aliquid; ut tibi, Antoni, Mancia, quom
audisset te censorem a M. Duronio de ambitu
postulatum,

fantastic not only for street performances but also, in a way, for us too. For example:

"What an idiot! The minute he started making money, he up and died!"

[A.] What's your relationship to this lady?
[B.] She's my wife.
[A.] Doh! Of course, looks just like you.

"He didn't die any of those times he was just *near* the water . . . !"

This type is sort of silly and, as I said, street-performerish. But it does sometimes have its place with us, too, such as when a not-stupid person says something in a seemingly stupid and funny way. An example is what Mancia told you, Antony, when you were Censor. He'd heard Marcus Duronius had brought you up on charges of electoral fraud, and quipped,

"Aliquando (*inquit*) tibi tuum negotium agere licebit."

[275] (*B.5.e*) Valde haec ridentur et hercule omnia quae a prudentibus per dissimulationem subabsurde salseque dicuntur. Ex quo genere est etiam non videri intellegere quod intellegas; ut Pontidius:

[A.] Qualem existimas qui in adulterio deprenditur?
[B.] Tardum!

Ut ego qui, in dilectu, Metello quom excusationem oculorum a me non acciperet et dixisset, "Tu igitur nihil vides?"

"You'll finally get to mind your own business!"

[275] (*B.5.e*) People crack up at these things. To be honest, they crack up at *everything* intelligent people say that's a funny non sequitur when they're speaking disingenuously. In this category belongs seeming to not understand something you do understand. For example, Pontidius:

[A.] In your view, what kind of man gets caught *in flagrante delicto*?
[B.] A slow one.

Another: Metellus was drafting men for the army and wouldn't accept my excuse of poor eyesight. "So, you can't see anything?" he asked. "Actually, I can," I said.

[276] Ego verò (*inquam*) a portā Esquilinā video villam tuam.

Ut illud Nasicae, qui quom ad poetam Ennium venisset eique ab ostio quaerenti Ennium ancilla dixisset domi non esse, Nasica sensit illam domini iussu dixisse et illum intus esse. Paucis post diebus, quom ad Nasicam venisset Ennius et eum ad ianuam quaereret, exclamat Nasica se domi non esse. Tum Ennius, "Quid? ¿Ego non cognosco vocem (*inquit*) tuam?" Hīc Nasica: "Homo es impudens!

Ego quom te quaererem, ancillae tuae credidi te domi non esse; ¿tu mihi non credis ipsi?"

[277] (*B.6*) Est bellum illud quoque ex quo is, qui dixit, irridetur in eo ipso genere quo dixit; ut quom Q. Opimius consularis, qui adulescen-

[276] "I can see your McMansion from the Esquiline Gate."

Another example is Nasica's classic. He'd come to the house of the poet Ennius and when he asked for Ennius at the front gate, the maid said he wasn't home. Nasica sensed she'd said that at her master's behest and that Ennius really *was* inside. A few days later, when Ennius came to Nasica's house and asked for him at the front door, Nasica shouted, "I'm not home!" Then Ennius said, "Huh? I recognize your voice!" "You sonofabitch," replied Nasica,

> "When I came looking for *you*, I believed your maid that you weren't home. Aren't you going to believe *me* myself?"

[277] (*B.6*) Another good type is when you zing a speaker with the same kind of joke he's just told. For example, Quintus Opimius was a

tulus male audisset, festivo homini Decio, qui
videretur esse mollior nec esset, dixisset, "Quid
tu, Decilla mea? Quando ad me venis cum tuā
colu et lanā?"

"Non pol (*inquit*) audeo. Nam me ad fa-
mosas vetuit mater accedere."

[278] (*B.7*) Salsa sunt etiam, quae habent suspicionem ridiculi absconditam. Quo in genere est
Siculi illud: cui quom familiaris quidam quer-
eretur, quod diceret uxorem suam suspendisse
se de ficu:

"Amabo te (*inquit*), da mihi ex istā arbore
quos seram surculos."

former Consul with a bad reputation as a teenager [*i.e., for being a man's boy toy*], and Decius was a fun guy who looked a bit gay, but wasn't. Opimius asked him, "How about it, Decilla sweetie? When are you coming over with your wool and sewing equipment?" "Lordie, I wouldn't dare," Decius replied.

"My mother told me to stay away from bad girls."

[278] (*B./*) Also funny are remarks that make you think they're hiding a joke. In this category belongs a well-known Sicilian joke. When a friend was wailing that his wife had hung herself from a fig tree, the Sicilian said,

"Any chance I could get a few cuttings from that tree to plant?"

In eodem genere est quod Catulus dixit cuidam oratori malo; qui, quom in epilogo misericordiam movisse se putaret, postquam adsedit, rogavit hunc videreturne misericordiam movisse. "Ac magnam quidem (*inquit*)!

> Hominem enim nullum puto esse tam durum cui non oratio tua miseranda visa sit."

[279] (*B.8*) Me quidem hercule etiam illa valde movent stomachosa et quasi submorosa ridicula—non quom a moroso dicuntur, tum enim non sal sed natura ridetur. In quo, ut mihi videtur, persalsum illud est apud Novium:

> [A.] "Quid ploras, pater?"
> [B.] "Mirum ni cantem? Condemnatus sum."

What Barker told a certain bad orator belongs in this same category. In the finale of a speech, the man thought he'd moved his audience to pity. Once he sat down, he asked Barker, "Do you think I moved them to pity?" "Oh *hell* yeah," replied Barker,

> "I don't think *anyone's* so hard-hearted that they didn't find your speech pitiful."

[279] (*B.8*) Personally, even jokes that are angry and (as it were) a bit cranky impress me. (Mind you, I don't mean "told by a cranky person," because in that case it's the person, not their jokes, that we laugh at.) A hilarious example in this category, in my view, is the one found in Novius:

> [A.] What are you crying for, dad?
> [B.] What, I should be singing? I just lost my case at court!

(*B.9*) Huic generi quasi contrarium est ridiculi genus patientis ac lenti; ut quom Cato percussus esset ab eo qui arcam ferebat; quom ille postea diceret, "Cave!" rogavit num

"quid aliud ferret praeter arcam."

[280] (*B.10*) Etiam stultitiae salsa est reprehensio; ut ille Siculus, cui praetor Scipio patronum causae dabat hospitem suum—hominem nobilem, sed admodum stultum:

"Quaeso (*inquit*), praetor, adversario meo da istum patronum, deinde mihi neminem dederis."

(*B.9*) Almost the opposite of this category is the category of patient, relaxed jokes. For example, Cato got banged into by a man carrying a heavy box. When the man then said, "Look out!" Cato asked,

"What, are you carrying anything else?"

[280] (*B.10*) Also funny is criticizing stupidity, as the Sicilian did. When Scipio was serving as a judge, he assigned him as legal counsel [*to interpret Roman law, of which the Sicilian was presumably ignorant*] a family friend who was well-born but really stupid. The Sicilian replied,

"With all due respect, your Honor, give that lawyer of yours to my opponent— then you won't need to assign anyone to me."

(*B.11*) Movent illa etiam, quae coniecturā explanantur longe aliter atquè sunt, sed acute atque concinne; ut, quom Scaurus accusaret Rutilium ambitūs quom ipse consul esset factus, ille repulsam tulisset, et in eius tabulis ostenderet litteras A F P R idque diceret esse: "Actum Fide P. Rutili," Rutilius autem: "Ante Factum, Post Relatum," C. Canius eques Romanus, quom Rufo adesset, exclamat neutrum illis litteris declarari. "Quid, ergo?" inquit Scaurus.

"Aemilius Fecit, Plectitur Rutilius!"

[281] (*B.12*) Ridentur etiam discrepantia:

"¿Quid huic abest—nisi res et virtus?"

(*B.11*) Also funny are things that an educated guess explains very differently than they really are, but in a way that's still clever and on point. For example, after Aemilius defeated Rutilius Rufus and won election as Consul, he prosecuted Rufus for electoral fraud. He showed Rutilius's account books; they had the letters A F R P marked on them, and he claimed they stood for "Accounts For Rutilius's Payoffs." Wrong, countered Rutilius, "Actions, Former; Recorded Presently." Since he was there in support of Rufus, Gaius Canius shouted out, "No, you're both wrong." "What do they mean, then?" inquired Aemilius.

"Aemilius? Fixer. Rutilius? Punished."

[281] (*B.12*) Inconsistencies also get laughs.

"That guy has it all—except money and redeeming qualities."

(*B.13*) Bella etiam est familiaris reprehensio quasi errantis; ut quom obiurgavit Albium Granius, quod, quom eius tabulis quiddam ab Albucio probatum videretur, et valde absoluto Scaevolā gauderet neque intellegeret

"contra suas tabulas esse iudicatum."

[282] (*B.14*) Huic similis est etiam admonitio in consilio dando familiaris; ut, quom patrono malo, quom vocem in dicendo obtudisset, suadebat Granius ut mulsum frigidum biberet simulac domum redisset, "Perdam" inquit "vocem, si id fecero!"

"Melius est (*inquit*) quàm reum."

(*B.13*) Nice, too, is pretending someone has made a mistake and criticizing them in a friendly fashion, such as when Granius rebuked White. White thought Albucius had used his [*White's*] account books as evidence to clinch his case in favor of Scaevola [*White's boss*]. When Scaevola was acquitted and White was celebrating joyously, Granius scolded him,

> "You ninny! Don't you understand that they acquitted *him*, but condemned your account books?"[44]

[282] (*B.14*) Similar to that is offering a friendly reminder when giving advice. For example, a not-very-good lawyer wound up hoarse from all his speaking, so Granius told him to go home and drink a cold digestif. "I'll ruin my voice if I do that!" he said.

> "Better that than your client."

[283] (*B.15*) Bellum etiam est, quom quid cuique sit consentaneum dicitur; ut quom Scaurus nonnullam haberet invidiam ex eo quod Phrygionis Pompei locupletis hominis bona sine testamento possederat, sederetque advocatus reo Bestiae, quom funus quoddam duceretur, accusator C. Memmius,

"Vide (*inquit*), Scaure! Mortuus rapitur, si potes esse possessor."

[284] (*B.16*) Sed ex his omnibus, nihil magis ridetur quàm quod est praeter expectationem, cuius innumerabilia sunt exempla; ut Appi maioris illud qui, in senatu quom ageretur de agris publicis et de lege Thoria, et peteretur Lucullus ab iis qui a pecore eius depasci agros publicos dicerent,

[283] (*B.15*) Also cute is when you point out someone's quirks. For example, people really envied Scaurus because he'd wound up in possession of a wealthy guy's property, and there hadn't been a will. When he came to a trial in an unrelated case, a funeral parade came passing by. As it did, the prosecutor, Memmius, quipped,

"Check it out, Scaurus—a dead man's being hustled off! Go see if you can get possession!"

[284] (*B.16*) But of all those categories, nothing gets bigger laughs than surprise jokes. Examples of them are endless. For instance, there was a debate in the senate about the legal implications of access to public farmlands, and Lucullus was attacked by those who claimed he was letting his cattle graze on those public lands.[45] Appius spoke up:

"Non est (*inquit*) Luculli pecus illud; erratis;"

—defendere Lucullum videbatur—

"Ego liberum puto esse: quālubet pascitur."

[285] Placet mihi illud etiam Scipionis illius qui Ti. Gracchum perculit. Quom ei M. Flaccus multis probris obiectis P. Mucium iudicem tulisset, "Eiero," inquit, "iniquus est." Quom esset admurmuratum,

"A! (*inquit*), P. C., non ego *mihi* illum iniquum eiero, verùm omnibus."

Ab hōc verò Crasso, nihil facetius quàm quom laesisset testis Silus Pisonem, quod se

"Those aren't Lucullus's cattle, you guys are wrong."

—he looked like he was defending Lucullus—

". . . I'd say they don't belong to *anyone*: they graze wherever they like."

[285] I also like the famous quip of a Scipio, the one who assassinated Tiberius Gracchus.[46] Flaccus kept blasting him in public repeatedly, and then proposed Scaevola as a judge to settle their dispute. "I reject him," said Scipio. "He's biased." When grumbling ensued, he quipped,

"I reject him as biased not against me, my fellow senators, but against everyone."

But nothing could be funnier than a quip of our Crassus here. A witness, Silus, had damaged Piso by saying he'd heard some nasty

in eum audisse dixisset: "Potest fieri (*inquit*) Sile, ut is, unde te audisse dicis, iratus dixerit." Adnuit Silus. "Potest etiam, ut tu non recte intellexeris." Id quoque toto capite adnuit, ut se Crasso daret. "Potest etiam fieri" inquit,

"Ut omnino, quod te audisse dicis, numquam audieris."

Hoc ita praeter expectationem accidit ut testem omnium risus obrueret.

Huius generis est plenus Novius, cuius ét iocus est familiaris—

"Sapiens, si algebis, tremes."

—ét alia permulta.

[286] (*B.17*) Saepe etiam facete concedas adversario id ipsum quod tibi ille detrahit; ut

remark about him. "It's possible, Silus," he said, "that your source was speaking in anger." Silus nodded. "It's possible, too, that you misunderstood him." He gave a big nod to that, which meant Crassus had him.

"It's possible, too, that what you say you heard, you never heard at all."

That came as such a surprise that the witness was drowned out by laughter on all sides.

Novius is full of this kind of thing. One's common:

"Guess what, Mr. 'Stoic': if it gets cold, you *will* shiver."

And there are tons of others.

[286] (*B.17*) It's also often funny to grant your opponent the very thing he's criticizing you for. For example, when some guttersnipe

C. Laelius, quom ei quidam malo genere natus diceret indignum esse suis maioribus,

"At hercule (*inquit*) tu tuis dignus."

(*B.18*) Saepe etiam sententiose ridicula dicuntur; ut M. Cincius, quo die legem "De donis et muneribus" tulit, quom C. Centho prodisset et satis contumeliose, "Quid fers, Cinciole?" quaesisset,

"Ut emas (*inquit*), Gai, si uti velis."

[287] (*B.19*) Saepe etiam salse quae fieri non possunt, optantur; ut M. Lepidus quom, ceteris se in campo exercentibus, ipse in herbā recubuisset:

kept saying Laelius didn't live up to his forefathers, he said,

"Well, by god, you live up to yours."

(*B.18*) Jokes are also often couched as nuggets of timeless wisdom. For example, the day Marcus Cincius proposed a bill [*restricting the acceptance of*] gifts, Gaius came over and asked, obnoxiously enough, "What's this (*winking*) 'bill' of yours asking for, my good Cincius?"

"That people pay for things they want, Gaius."[47]

[287] (*B.19*) Impossible wishes are often funny, too. For example, when everyone else was doing their physical training in the Campus Martius and Lepidus was kicking back on the grass, he quipped,

"Vellem hoc esset (*inquit*) laborare!"

(*B.20*) Salsum est etiam quaerentibus et quasi percontantibus lente respondere quod nolint; ut censor Lepidus, quom M. Antistio Pyrgensi equum ademisset, amicique quom vociferarentur et quaererent quid ille patri suo responderet cur ademptum sibi equum diceret, quom "optimus colonus," quom "parcissimus," "modestissimus," "frugalissimus" esset,

"me istorum (*inquit*) nihil credere."

[288] (*B.21–23*) Colliguntur a Graecis alia nonnulla—execrationes, admirationes, minationes—sed haec ipsa nimis mihi videor in multa genera discripsisse. Nam illa, quae verbi

"I wish *this* counted as working out."

(*B.20*) When people keep asking you a question and are practically badgering you for a reply, it's also funny to slowly give them an answer they don't want. For example, when Lepidus was Censor, he confiscated the [*state-supplied*] horse of Marcus Antistius of Pyrgi. Antistius's friends got all upset and kept asking, "What should our friend tell his dad about why his horse has gotten confiscated? Given that he's a first-rate Roman, excellent with money, incredibly modest, fantastic at controlling costs...." Lepidus replied,

"That I don't believe any of that."

[288] (*B.21–23*) The Greeks collect some other types—curses, expressions of amazement, threats—but I think I've already overcatego rized the jokes in my second group, since the

ratione et vi continentur, certa fere ac definita
sunt; quae plerùmque, ut ante dixi, laudari
magis quàm rideri solent.

[289] Haec (*B.*) autem, quae sunt in re et ipsā
sententiā, partibus sunt innumerabilia, generi-
bus pauca. (*1*) Expectationibus enim decipiendis, et (*2*) naturis—aliorum irridendis, ipsorum
ridicule indicandis—et (*3*) similitudine turpioris, et (*4*) dissimulatione, et (*5*) subabsurda
dicendo, et (*6*) stulta reprehendendo, risūs mov-
entur. Itaque, imbuendus est is qui iocose volet
dicere, quasi naturā quadam aptā ad haec genera et moribus, ut ad cuiusque modi genus ridiculi vultus etiam accommodetur; qui quidem
quó severior est et tristior—ut in te, Crasse—
hóc illa quae dicuntur salsiora videri solent.

first group, which are created by the expression and meaning of language, are basically specific and limited (and like I said, they tend to win admiration rather than laughter).

[289] My (*B.*) group, though, which depends on the thing and idea itself, can be divided into infinite species, though only a few types. You see, laughter is provoked by (*1*) surprises, (*2*) making fun of other people's quirks or giving a funny clue as to our own, (*3*) comparing a thing to something worse, (*4*) disingenuousness, (*5*) non sequiturs, and (*6*) criticizing stupidity. Hence, those who want to master jokes for public speaking need to be imbued with a certain—almost innate—sense of humor and a personality that's suited to these types, so that their facial expression can also be made to match each type of joke. And usually, the sterner and more serious that expression is—like yours, Crassus the funnier the things you say seem to be.

[290] Sed iam tu, Antoni—qui in hōc deversorio sermonis mei libenter adquieturum te esse dixisti—tamquam in Pomptinum devertĕris: neque amoenum neque salubrem locum. Censeo ut satis diu te putes requiesse et iter reliquum conficere pergas.

ANTONIUS

Ego verò, atque hilare quidem a te acceptus (*inquit*) et cúm doctior per te, túm etiam audacior factus iam ad iocandum. Non enim vereor ne quis me in isto genere leviorem iam putet, quoniam quidem tu Fabricios mihi auctores et Africanos, Maximos, Catones, Lepidos protulisti.

Final Remarks

[290] Well, Antony, you did say you'd be glad to take a rest in this discourse-motel of mine, but it looks like you actually took a pit stop in the Pomptine Marshes—not the nicest place, or very conducive to your health. I think you should decide you've rested up enough, check out, and finish the rest of your trip.

ANTONY

That I'll do, thanks to such a fun and good reception from you. And, because of you, I'll do so better informed and more confident in my joking. You see, I'm not afraid of looking like a lightweight in this area anymore, now that you've produced Fabriciuses and Africanuses and Maximuses and Catos and Lepiduses as my authorities.

Cicero was hunted down and murdered twelve years after publishing this treatise, his master-piece. The goon squad was sent by Mark Antony, a politician-turned-warlord that Cicero had roasted in a merciless series of political speeches called The Philippics—*and, funny enough, the grandson of the Antony we just met. The thugs cut Cicero's head and hands off and hung them up for display in the Forum, a warning to all.*

In the ensuing decades, Rome transformed from a republic, in which free speech mattered, to an empire, where it didn't. For better or worse, the art of persuasive speaking remained the bedrock of all liberal education in Rome. About 80 years after Cicero's death, Quintilian was born in Roman Spain. By the end of his career, he had risen to occupy the world's first chair of Latin rhetoric in Rome. An extract from his own masterpiece, The Education of the Orator, *follows.*

Like many dictators, Rome's first emperor, Octavian (63 BCE—14 CE), took to calling himself The Leader (princeps) *upon consolidating his power. The Senate, however, voted him the nickname* The Reverend (Augustus)—*a good example of an unintentionally funny name, like Papa Doc—and it eventually replaced his proper name. He makes an appearance several times in Quintilian's treatise.*

ON THE ART OF HUMOR

Quintilianus, *Institutio Oratoria*, Liber 6.3

[1] Huic diversa, virtus quae risum iudicis movendo ét illos tristīs solvit affectūs et animum ab intentione rerum frequenter avertit et aliquando etiam reficit et a satietate vel a fatigatione renovat.

Quanta sit autem in ea difficultas, vél duo maximi oratores—alter Graecae, alter Latinae eloquentiae princeps—docent. [2] Nam plerique Demostheni facultatem defuisse huius rei credunt, Ciceroni modum. Nec videri potest

ON THE ART OF HUMOR

Quintilian, *The Education of the Orator*,
Book 6.3

Why It's Hard to Go for Laughs

[1] Yet another skill [*that orators should culti-
vate*] is getting the jury to laugh. Doing that
breaks up their upset emotions, takes their mind
off the facts, and sometimes even snaps them
out of it and gives them a fresh start when
they're tired or bored.

That said, the two greatest orators in
history—one the leading light of Greek eloquence, the other of Latin—are a study in how
truly hard it is, [2] because lots of people think
that Demosthenes had no ability to do it and
Cicero none to resist it. It's impossible that

noluisse Demosthenes, cuius pauca admodum dicta—nec sane ceteris eius virtutibus
respondentia—palam ostendunt non *displicuisse*
illi iocos, sed non contigisse. [3] Noster verò
non solum extra iudicia sed in ipsis etiam orationibus habitus est nimius risūs affectator.
Mihi quidem, sive id recte iudico sive amore
immodico praecipui in eloquentiā viri labor,
mira quaedam in eo videtur fuisse urbanitas.
[4] Nam ét in sermone cotidiano multa ét in al-
tercationibus et interrogandis testibus plura
quàm quisquam dixit facete, et illa ipsa quae
sunt in Verrem dicta frigidius aliis adsignavit
et testimonii loco posuit, ut, quó sunt magis
vulgaria, eó sit credibilius illa non ab oratore
ficta, sed passim esse iactata. [5] ¡Utinamque
libertus eius Tiro, aut alius, quisquis fuit, qui

Demosthenes was uninterested in it, because the very few quips he does have—which are at odds with all his other skills—clearly show it's not that he disliked jokes, they just weren't any good; [3] whereas people regarded our man Cicero as an excessive laugh-getter, and not only in normal life but even in his public speeches. Personally, for what it's worth—whether it's because I'm right or because I'm swayed by my outsized enthusiasm for the man who towers over eloquence—I think he did have a certain amazing urbanity in him, [4] because he cracked lots of jokes in his everyday discourse and more of them than anyone else in legal debates and examining witnesses. Even the misfires he launched at Verres he attributed to others and treated as witness testimony, so that the more hackneyed they are, the easier it is to believe that Cicero didn't come up with them, and that they were instead common coin.[48] [5] I wish his freedman Tiro (or whoever it was that published

tres hac de re libros edidit, parcius dictorum numero indulsissent et plus iudicii in eligendis quàm in congerendis studii adhibuissent! Minus obiectus calumniantibus foret, qui tamen nunc quoque, ut in omni eius ingenio, facilius quod reici quàm quod adici possit invenient.

[6] Affert autem rei summam difficultatem primum quod ridiculum dictum plerùmque falsum est, saepe ex industriā depravatum, praeterea semper humile, numquam honorificum: tum varia hominum iudicia in eo quod non ratione aliquā sed motu animi quodam nescio an enarrabili iudicatur. [7] Neque enim ab ullo satis explicari puto (lìcet multi temptaverint) *unde* risus, qui non solum facto aliquo dictove sed interdum quodam etiam corporis tactu lacessitur. Praeterea, non unā ratione moveri solet: neque enim acute tantùm ac venuste,

his three books on the topic) had been stingier about the *number* of quips and used a little more judgment in selecting than enthusiasm for collecting them! Then Cicero would've been less of a target for his critics, who will, as with every other area he was good at, nevertheless even now more easily find something to reject than to add in.

[6] Moreover, a first major problem with mastering humor is that a joke is typically untrue, often deliberately slanted, and always demeaning and never flattering. Second, people's reactions vary, since reactions in this domain are based not on logic but on some primal emotion. [7] You see, I don't think anyone's really explained—though many have tried—where laughter comes from, since it can be provoked not just by some action or word, but sometimes by certain kinds of physical contact, too. Moreover, there's no one thing that arouses it: it's not just clever or cute remarks and actions that

sed stulte iracunde timide dicta ac facta ridentur, ideoque anceps eius rei ratio est, quod a de-
risu non procul abest risus. [8] Habet enim, ut
Cicero dicit, sedem in deformitate aliquā et
turpitudine: quae quom in *aliis* demonstrantur,
"urbanitas," quom in ipsos dicentīs reccidunt,
"stultitia" vocatur.

Quom videatur autem res levis et quae a
scurris, mimis, insipientibus denique saepe
moveatur, tamen habet vim nescio an imperi-
osissimam et cui repugnari minime potest. [9]
Erumpit etiam invitis saepe, nec vultūs modo ac
vocis exprimit confessionem, sed totum corpus
vi suā concutit. Rerum autem saepe, ut dixi,
maximarum momenta vertit, ut quom odium
iramque frequentissime frangat.

get laughed at; stupid, angry, or frightened ones do, too. And that explains why humor is risky, since *wit* is so close to *twit*. [8] You see, as Cicero says [*in 236*], laughter has its home in some ugliness and disgrace. And it's called "urbanity" when you draw attention to it in others, but when it boomerangs back at the speaker, it's called "stupidity."

What's more, laughter seems like a minor thing, something that any stand-up comedian, street performer, or idiot can get. Nevertheless, it does have a certain overpowering and conquering force, where all resistance is futile. [9] It oftentimes erupts from us even against our will, not only squeezing a confession from the face and voice but even rocking the whole body forcefully. As I said, though [*in section 1*], it can change the course of the most serious matters, since it zaps anger and animosity with great frequency.[49]

[10] Documento sunt iuvenes Tarentini, qui multa de rege Pyrrho sequius inter cenam locuti, quom rationem facti reposcerentur et neque negari res neque defendi posset, risu sunt et oportuno ioco elapsi. Namque unus ex iis—

"Immo (*inquit*), nisi lagona defecisset, occidissemus te."

—eāque urbanitate tota est invidia criminis dissoluta.

[11] Verùm hoc quidquid est, ut non ausim dicere carere omnino arte, quia nonnullam observationem habet suntque ad id pertinentia ét a Graecis ét a Latinis composita praecepta, ita plane affirmo praecipue positum esse in (*1*) naturā et in (*2*) occasione.

[10] The case of those teenagers in Tarentum proves it. At a dinner party, they'd said a lot of really nasty things about King Pyrrhus. When they were brought in to explain themselves, and since there was no denying or defending it, they escaped with a laugh and a well-timed joke. One of them quipped,

"Naw, man, if we hadn't run out of booze, we would've killed you."

—and that witticism melted away all the hard feelings over the charge.

[11] Whatever humor is—though I won't quite say there's no art to it whatsoever, since it does entail some structure, and since Greek and Latin authors alike have composed rules for it—I will still state for the record that it is primarily a product of (*1*) genetics and (*2*) the right opportunity.

[12] (*1*) Porro, natura non tantùm in hoc valet, ut acutior quis atque habilior sit ad inveniendum (nam id sane doctrinā possit augeri), sed inest proprius quibusdam decor in habitu ac vultu, ut eadem illa minus, alio dicente, urbana esse videantur. [13] (*2*) Occasio verò ét in rebus est, cuius est tanta vis ut saepe adiuti eā non indocti modo sed etiam rustici salse dicant, ét in eo, quid aliquis dixerit prior; sunt enim longe venustiora omnia in respondendo quàm in provocando.

[14] Accedit difficultati quod eius rei nulla exercitatio est, nulli praeceptores. Itaque, in conviviis et sermonibus multi dicaces, quia in hoc usu cotidiano proficimus: oratoria urbanitas rara, nec ex arte propriā sed ab hac consuetudine commodata.

[12] (*1*) Moreover, genetics don't merely determine whether a person is wittier and quicker at coming up with ideas (because teaching really *could* improve that); no, some people just intrinsically have a special look about them—the way they move, their face—such that the same jokes don't seem as funny when someone else tells them. [13] (*2*) The right opportunity, though—which is so powerful that it often helps not only uneducated people, but even hillbillies to crack jokes—hinges on both situations and also on what a prior speaker says, because every quip is much more fun as a comeback than a provocation.

[14] Another thing that makes humor hard [*see section 6*] is that there are no practice lessons for it, no teachers. The upshot is that many people are great at sick burns at parties and in conversation because everyday life experience lets us get better at it, but wittiness in public

[15] (Nihil autem vetabat ét componi mate-
rias in hoc idoneas, ut controversiae permixtis
salibus fingerentur, vel res proponi singulas ad
iuvenum talem exercitationem. [16] Quin, ipsae
illae ("diasyrticae" vocantur) quas certis diebus
festae licentiae dicere solebamus, si paulùm
adhibitā ratione fingerentur aut aliquid in his
serium quoque esset admixtum, plurimum po-
terant utilitatis afferre: quae nunc iuvenum
versibus ludentium exercitatio est.)

[17] Pluribus autem nominibus in eādem re
vulgò utimur: quae tamen si diducas, suam
quandam propriam vim ostendent.

(*1*) Nam ét "urbanitas" dicitur, qua quidem
significari video sermonem praeferentem in verbis et sono et usu proprium quendam gustum

speaking is rare, and it borrows from those routines instead of having its own set of rules.

[15] (Still, nothing's ever stopped anyone from creating instructional materials suitable for it, such as mock debates that would be genuinely funny or special prompts to drill students in it. [16] It's the opposite, actually. If we systematized them a bit or added a little seriousness to the mix, one thing that could be really useful are those cut-downs (the "diasyrtics") that we used to take turns exchanging on "anything goes" days. At the moment, they're just a one-upping game for students having fun.)

Six Different Kinds of Humor

[17] At any rate, we generally use a number of different names for the same thing [*humor*], and if we look at them separately, each one will reveal its own special properties.

(*1*) One is "urbanity," which in my experience means speech whose words, sounds, and

Urbis et sumptam ex conversatione doctorum tacitam eruditionem, denique cui contraria sit rusticitas.

[18] (2) "Venustum" esse quod cum gratiā quadam et venere dicatur apparet.

(3) "Salsum" in consuetudine pro ridiculo tantùm accipimus: naturā non utique hoc est, quamquam ét ridicula esse oporteat salsa.

(3.a) Nam ét Cicero omne quod salsum sit ait esse Atticorum, non quia sunt maxime ad risum compositi,

(3.b) ét Catullus, quom dicit:

♫"Nulla est in corpore mica salis, "♫

usage lead with an unmistakable "city" [*urbs*] flavor and a quiet sophistication picked up from being around educated people; its opposite is "countrified speech" [*rusticitas*]."[50]

[18] (2) "Charming" [*venustum*] obviously means something said with a certain grace and "charm" [*Venus*].

(3) We only say "salty" or "zesty" [*salsus*] in ordinary speech of something funny. It's not necessarily funny by nature, though anything salty should also be funny, too.[51] I say this because:

(*3.a*) Cicero says [*in Orator 90*] that everything that's "salty" is a hallmark of Attic Greek writers (and he doesn't mean that they're maximally geared toward laughter), and

(*3.b*) Catullus, when he says [*poem 86.4*],

♫"There's not a grain of salt in her body"♫

non hoc dicit, "nihil" in corpore eius esse "ridiculum."

[19] Salsum igitur erit quod non erit insulsum, velut quoddam simplex orationis condimentum, quod sentitur latente iudicio velut palato, excitatque et a taedio defendit orationem. Sales enim, út ille in cibis paulo liberalius adspersus—si tamen non sit immodicus—affert aliquid propriae voluptatis, íta hi quoque in dicendo habent quiddam quod nobis faciat audiendi sitim.

[20] (4) "Facetum" quoque non tantùm circa ridicula opinor consistere; neque enim diceret Horatius facetum carminis genus naturā concessum esse Vergilio. Decoris hanc magis et excultae cuiusdam elegantiae appellationem puto. Ideoque, in epistulis Cicero haec Bruti refert verba:

—doesn't mean there's nothing *funny* in her body.

[19] Hence "salty" [*salsum*] must mean "not bland" [*insulsum*]. It's like a basic flavor enhancer for our speech, one our minds take in imperceptibly the way our taste buds do, and it keeps speech from getting boring. You see, just as real salt [*sal*] enhances our enjoyment of food when it's given a good sprinkling (without overdoing it, though), so too do jokes [*sales*] possess a certain something that makes us thirsty to listen.

[20] (4) "Witty" [*facetum*] is another one that I don't think means just "funny." If it did, Horace wouldn't say [*Satires* 1.10.44–45] that Nature granted Virgil a "witty" style of poetry [*in the* Eclogues]. In my view, the word rather denotes charm and a certain polished elegance. Hence in his letters [*fragmentary letters 17.2, ed. Watt*], Cicero quotes Brutus:

"¡Né illi sunt pedes faceti ac per delicias ingredientis mollius!"

Quod convenit cum illo Horatiano:

♫"Molle atque facetum
Vergilio."♫

[21] (5) "Iocum" verò id accipimus quod est contrarium serio. . . . nam ét fingere et terrere et promittere interim iocus est.

(6) "Dicacitas" sine dubio a dicendo, quod est omni generi commune, ducta est; proprie tamen significat sermonem cum risu aliquos incessentem. Ideo Demosthenen urbanum fuisse dicunt, dicacem negant.

"Yessir, *those* are the cadences of a wit, of a man gayly prancing in!"

And that accords with Horace's line [*Satire* 1.10.44–45],

♫"Prancing, witty: that's Virgil for you!"♫

[21] (5) By contrast, we take a "joke" [*iocus*] to be the opposite of "serious." [. . . *some words missing here* . . .] You see, making up stories, scaring people, and making promises are all jokes at times.

(6) "Being a jerk" [*dicacitas*] is obviously derived from *dicere* ["to say"], which is the common element in every kind of humor, though properly it means "to sneer." That's why people say Demosthenes was urbane, but they don't say he was a jerk.[52]

[22] Proprium autem materiae de qua nunc loquimur est ridiculum, ideoque haec tota disputatio a Graecis "περὶ γελοίου" inscribitur. Eius prima divisio traditur eadem quae est omnis orationis, ut sit positum in rebus ac verbis. [23] Usus autem maxime triplex: aut enim (*1*) ex aliis risum petimus, aut (*2*) ex nobis, aut (*3*) ex rebus mediis. (*1*) Aliena aut reprendimus, aut refutamus, aut elevamus, aut repercutimus, aut eludimus. (*2*) Nostra ridicule indicamus et, ut verbo Ciceronis utar, dicimus aliqua "subabsurda." Namque eadem quae si imprudentibus excidant stulta sunt, si simulamus, venusta creduntur. [24] (*3*) Tertium est genus, ut īdem dicit, in decipiendis expectationibus, dictis aliter

Humor as a Whole, and Its Uses

[22] All that said, the proper object of our current discussion is humor, which is why the Greeks title the whole subject *peri geloiou* [*on humor*]. [23] We're told its main division, like that of all oratory, is into humor that's based on language versus humor based on things [*Cicero 239*], and it has three main uses: we want to make people laugh at (*1*) someone else, (*2*) us ourselves, or (*3*) neutral things. In (*1*), we criticize, expose, disparage, mimic, or dodge other people's words or situations. In (*2*), we give our own the funny treatment, and we can utter some "non sequiturs" (to use Cicero's name for them [*in 274 and 289*]). You see, things that sound stupid when they slip out accidentally are thought charming when we feign them. [24] Category (*3*), as Cicero also says [*in 289*], lies in surprises, misunderstanding words, and

accipiendis, ceteris, quae neutram personam contingunt ideoque a me "media" dicuntur.

[25] Item ridicula aut (*A*) facimus aut (*B*) dicimus. (*A.1*) Facto risus conciliatur interim admixtā gravitate; ut M. Caelius praetor, quom sellam eius curulem consul Isauricus fregisset, alteram posuit loris intentam (dicebatur autem consul a patre flagris aliquando caesus); (*A.2*) interim sine respectu pudoris, ut in illā pyxide Caelianā, quod neque oratori neque ulli viro gravi conveniat. [26] (Idem autem de vultu gestuque ridiculo dictum sit: in quibus est quidem sua gratia, sed maior quom captare risum non videntur; nihil enim est iis quae sicuti salsa dicuntur insulsius. Quamquam autem gratiae plurimum dicentis severitas affert, fitque

everything else that doesn't affect either party, and hence I call them "neutral."

[25] Another point is that humor lies in either (*A*) our actions or (*B*) our words. (*A.1*) An action wins laughter by mixing in seriousness. For example, Marcus Caelius was serving as a judge. When the Consul, Isauricus, destroyed his barrister chair [*as a public sign of his disbarment*], Caelius replaced it with one whose webbing was made of whips (rumor had it that the Consul had once earned a whipping from his father). (*A.2*) Otherwise, an action wins laughter by indecency, such as with Caelius's notorious "box," which no respectable orator or gentleman should have anything to do with.[53] [26] (The same should be said for funny faces and gestures. Yes, they have their appeal, but more so when they aren't obviously angling for laughs, since nothing's as unfunny as a joke that's told as explicitly funny. And although deadpan delivery does maximize charm and the

ridiculum id ipsum quod qui dicit illa, non ridet, est tamen interim ét aspectus ét habitus oris ét gestus non inurbanus, quom iis modus contigit.)

[27] (*B*) Id porro quod dicitur aut est (*B.1*) lascivum et hilare, qualia Gabbae pleraque, aut (*B.2*) contumeliosum, qualia nuper Iuni Bassi, aut (*B.3*) asperum, qualia Cassi Severi, aut (*B.4*) lene, qualia Domiti Afri. [28] Rēfert, his ubi quis utatur. Nam in convictibus et cotidiano sermone lasciva humilibus, hilaria omnibus convenient. Laedere numquam velimus, longeque absit illud propositum, potius amicum quàm dictum perdendi. In hac quidem pugnā forensi, malim mihi lenibus uti licere. Nonnumquam ét contumeliose ét aspere dicere in adversarios permissum est, quom accusare etiam palam et caput alterius iuste petere concessum sit. Sed hīc quoque, tamen, inhumana

fact alone that the speaker isn't laughing becomes funny, nevertheless from time to time there's a look, a facial expression, and a gesture that's not without urbanity, provided it's kept in due limits.)

[27] (B) The jokes we tell can be (B.1) risqué and corny, like a lot of Gabba's; (B.2) insulting, like Junius Bassus's recently; (B.3) harsh, like Cassius Severus's; or (B.4) lighthearted, like Domitius Afer's.[54] [28] What matters is when and where they're told. At social gatherings and around the water cooler, risqué jokes will suit the lower classes, while corny jokes will be fine for everyone. We should never want to cause hurt, and let's keep far from the idea that "it's better to lose a friend than a jest." In our court battles, I'd rather get to use lighthearted jokes. Since we're entitled to make accusations openly and to legitimately seek the death penalty, it is sometimes allowable to get tough on opponents and insult them, but even then it usually looks

videri solet fortunae insectatio, vel quod culpā caret vel quod reccidere etiam in ipsos qui obiecerunt potest. Primum itaque considerandum est ét quis et in qua causā et apud quem et in quem et quid dicat.

[29] Oratori minime convenit distortus vultus gestusque, quae in mimis rideri solent. Dicacitas etiam scurrilis et scaenica huic personae alienissima est; obscenitas, verò, non a verbis tantùm abesse debet sed etiam a significatione. Nam siquando obici potest, non in ioco exprobranda est. [30] Oratorem praeterea út dicere urbane volo, íta videri affectare id plane nolo. Quapropter, ne dicet quidem salse quotiens poterit, et dictum potius aliquando perdet quàm minuet auctoritatem. [31] Nec accusatorem

callous to go after someone's luck in life, because it's not their fault or because it can even back-fire on the attacker. The first things to take stock of, therefore, are who is doing the speaking, what the legal case is, who the judge presiding is, and who the opponent is.

[29] The orator must have absolutely no truck with the exaggerated facial expressions and gestures that street performers get their laughs with. The sneering of stand-up comedians is completely alien to his persona. Obscenity, too, should be absent not only from his language but even from his meaning. If an allegation of obscenity ever can be made, it should not be couched as a laughing matter. [30] Furthermore, just as I do want the orator to speak urbanely, I also don't want him to look like he's trying too hard. Accordingly, he shall not crack a joke every time he can, and on occasion he'll forgo a jest rather than diminish his authority. [31] Moreover, no one will put up

autem atroci in causā nec patronum in misera-
bili iocantem feret quisquam. Sunt etiam iudices quidam tristiores quàm ut risum libenter
patiantur.

[32] Solet interim accidere ut id quod in adversarium dicimus aut in iudicem conveniat aut
in nostrum quoque litigatorem, quamquam
aliqui reperiuntur qui ne id quidem quod in
ipsos reccidere possit evitent. Quod fecit Longus Sulpicius, qui, quom ipse foedissimus esset,
ait eum contra quem iudicio liberali aderat ne
faciem quidem habere liberi hominis; cui re-
spondens Domitius Afer,

"Ex tui (*inquit*) animi sententiā, Longe,
qui malam faciem habet, ¿liber non est?"

[33] Vitandum etiam ne petulans, ne superbum,
ne loco, ne tempore alienum, ne praeparatum et
domo allatum videatur quod dicimus; nam

with a prosecutor cracking jokes in the case of a heinous crime or with a defense attorney in a heartbreaking one. Some judges, too, are too serious to willingly tolerate laugher.

[32] It sometimes happens that a quip we make about an opponent also applies to the judge or our own client; and yet you find some who don't even avoid a quip that can boomerang back on themselves. An example is Sulpicius Longus. He was pug ugly himself, but at a hearing on free-versus-slave status he said his opponent ". . . doesn't even have the *face* of a free man!" Domitius Afer fired back,

> "Do you really and truly think, Longus, that *any* horse-faced man must be a slave?"

[33] We also must not let a quip we make appear flippant, arrogant, inappropriate, rehearsed, or cooked up in advance, because, as I said earlier,

adversùs miseros, sicut supra dixeram, inhuma-
nus est iocus. Sed quidam ita sunt receptae auc-
toritatis ac notae verecundiae ut nocitura sit in
eos dicenti petulantia; nam de amicis iam praeceptum est. [34] Illud non ad oratoris consilium
sed ad hominis pertinet: lacessat hōc modo
quem laedere sit periculosum, ne aut inimicitiae
graves insequantur aut turpis satisfactio.

Male etiam dicitur quod in plurīs convenit,
si aut nationes totae incessantur aut ordines aut
condicio aut studia multorum. [35] Ea quae
dicet vir bonus, omnia salvā dignitate ac
verecundiā dicet; nimium enim risūs pretium
est si probitatis impendio constat.

a joke at the expense of those less fortunate is cruel. Moreover, some people command such authority and respect that any flippancy toward them will only harm the speaker. (On the topic of friends, I've already had my say [*in section 28*].) [34] And that point pertains not so much to orators as to human beings in general: if someone is dangerous to offend, you'd best tease them in a way that doesn't lead to either real hatred or to you having to issue a groveling apology.

Generalizations are another bad idea, where you attack whole groups based on ethnic identity, class, status, or activities the masses enjoy. [35] A gentleman will say what he will contingent on maintaining his dignity and self-respect. A laugh is overpriced if it comes at the cost of integrity.

Unde autem concilietur risus et quibus ex locis peti soleat, difficillimum dicere. Nam si species omnīs persequi velimus, nec modum reperiemus et frustra laborabimus. [36] Neque enim minus numerosi sunt loci ex quibus haec dicta quàm illi ex quibus eae quas "sententias" vocamus ducuntur, neque alii. Nam hīc quoque est inventio et elocutio, atque ipsius elocutionis vis alia in verbis, alia in figuris.

[37] Risūs igitur oriuntur aut (*1*) ex corpore eius in quem dicimus, aut (*2*) ex animo, qui factis ab eo dictisque colligitur, aut (*3*) ex iis quae sunt extra posita. Intra haec enim est omnis vituperatio: quae si gravius posita sit, severa est,

How to Get a Laugh and Win the Room: Targets and Techniques

It would be impossible to list all the methods of winning laughter and the sources people resort to for it, since we'd be wasting our time and never get to the end if we try to chase down every single type. [36] You see, the sources of jokes are no less numerous—and no different— than the sources of what we call "timeless nuggets of wisdom" [*sententiae*]. Here too, we find brainstorming [*inventio*] and style of presenta tion [*elocutio*], as well as the effectiveness of that style, half of which comes from language and half from rhetorical tricks.

[37] Laughs, then, come about from (*1*) the body of the person we're targeting, (*2*) his mind, as inferred from his behavior, or (*3*) external cir- cumstances. Every attack falls under one of these headings: if the attack is made in earnest, it's brutalizing; if you use a soft touch, it's funny.

si levius, ridicula. Haec aut (*1*) ostenduntur aut
(*2*) narrantur aut (*3*) dicto notantur.

[38] (*1*) Rarum est ut oculis subicere con-
tingat, ut fecit C. Iulius, qui—quom Helvio
Manciae saepius obstrepenti sibi diceret, "Iam
ostendam qualis sis!" isque plane instaret in-
terrogatione qualem tandem se ostensurus
esset—digito demonstravit imaginem Galli in
scuto Cimbrico pictam, cui Mancia tum simil-
limus est visus. (Tabernae autem erant circa
Forum ac scutum illud signi gratiā positum.)

[39] (*2*) Narrare quae salsa sint, imprimis est
subtile et oratorium, ut Cicero "Pro Cluentio"
narrat de Caepasio atque Fabricio, aut M. Caelius

You can (*1*) *demonstrate* all these things, (*2*) *tell* of them, or (*3*), with a zinger, *brand* and *sear* them into memory.

[38] (*1*) It's rare to get a chance to show it, the way Caesar did [*meaning the main speaker of Cicero's dialogue, section 266*]. When Helvius Mancia wouldn't stop interrupting him, he said, "Now I'm going to show you the kind of guy you are." And when Mancia kept pestering him—"C'mon, why dontcha? What exactly are you going to show I'm like?"—Caesar pointed to the image of a Gaul painted on a Cimbric shield that looked exactly the way Mancia did at that moment. (There were shops around the Forum and the shield had been set up there as a monument.)

[39] (*2*) Telling a funny story is an especially subtle trick of the oratorical trade; examples include Cicero's story of Caepasius and [*his client*] Fabricius in his speech *In Defense of Cluentius* [*sections 57–58*] and Marcus Caelius's

de illā D. Laeli collegaeque eius in provinciam festinantium contentione. Sed in his omnibus, cúm elegans et venusta exigitur tota expositio, túm id festivissimum est quod adicit orator. [40] Nam ét a Cicerone sic est Fabrici fuga illa condīta:

"Itaque, quom callidissime se putaret dicere, et quom illa verba gravissima ex intimo artificio deprompsisset,

'Respicite, iudices, hominum fortunas! Respicite C. Fabrici senectutem!'

—quom hoc 'respicite' ornandae orationis causā saepe dixisset, 'respexit' ipse—at Fabricius a subselliis, demisso capite, discesserat!"

178

story [*in a speech now lost*] of the famous fight between Decimus Laelius and his colleague as they hurried off to their province. In all such cases, not only is the entire anecdote crafted with elegance and charm, but the most winsome parts are the fillips the orator adds to it. [40] For example, here's how Cicero peppered[55] Fabricius's famous getaway:

> . . . and so, when Caepasius thought he was doing a *genius*-level job of speaking, and, from the bottom of his bag of tricks he'd pulled out these impressive words—
>
> (*imitating the voice of Caepasius, Fabricius's lawyer*) "Have some regard, gentlemen of the jury, for the reversals of fortune that human beings endure! Have some regard for Gaius Fabricius's old age!"

—et cetera quae adiecit (nam est notus locus), quom in re hoc solum esset, Fabricium a iudicio recessisse;

[41] ét Caelius, cúm omnia venustissime finxit, túm illud ultimum:

"Hic subsecutus quomodo transierit— utrum rati an piscatorio navigio—nemo sciebat. Siculi quidem—ut sunt lascivi et dicaces—aiebant ¡in delphino sedisse et sic tamquam Ariona transvectum!"

> —and when he'd kept repeating the "Have some regard!" to pump up his speech, he "regarded" the scene—but Fabricius had pulled his collar up and slunk away![56]

And so on, with all the other fillips (it's a famous passage)—when in reality, all that really happened is that Fabricius had left the court.

[41] Caelius too shaped his whole anecdote with supreme irony, especially the last bit:

> "He did follow, but how did he make it across—Raft? Fishing boat? Nobody knew. If you asked the Sicilians (who do, you know, love to make obnoxious jokes), they'd say he saddled up a dolphin and rode on over, Arion-style."[57]

[42] (*3*) In narrando autem Cicero consistere facetias putat, dicacitatem in iaciendo. Mire fuit in hōc genere venustus Afer Domitius, cuius orationibus complures huiusmodi narrationes insertae reperiuntur, sed dictorum quoque ab eodem urbane sunt editi libri.

[43] (Illud quoque genus est, positum non in hac veluti iaculatione dictorum et inclusa breviter urbanitate, sed in quodam longiore actu, quod de L. Crasso contra Brutum Cicero in secundo "De Oratore" libro et aliis quibusdam locis narrat. [44] Nam quom Brutus, in accusatione Cn. Planci, excitatis duobus lectoribus ostendisset contraria L. Crassum (patronum eius) in oratione quam "De colonia Narbonensi"

On Wisecracks (Quips and Comebacks)

[42] (3) Anyway, Cicero [*in* Orator 87] thinks wit lies in storytelling, while being a jerk lies in sniping. Domitius Afer was amazingly smooth in the first category—scads of his stories of this type are found as insertions in his speeches—but whole books of his wisecracks have been published, too.

[43] (There's also this one more category, too, that isn't a matter of wisecrack-sniping and concentrated witticisms but of a certain longer development. Cicero talks about it in *On the Ideal Orator* book 2 [*section 223*] and a few other places in regard to Crassus's rough treatment of Brutus. [44] You see, Brutus had brought a charge against Gnaeus [*sic: Cicero calls him Gaius*] Plancus, and at the trial he summoned two readers who demonstrated some inconsistencies—namely, that in his speech on the colony of Narbo, Plancus's lawyer,

habuerat suasisse iis quae "De lege Servilia"
dixerat, tres excitavit ét ipse lectores, iisque
patris eius "Dialogos" dedit legendos; quorum
quom in Privernati unus, alter in Albano,
tertius in Tiburti sermonem habitum com-
plecteretur, requirebat ubi essent eae possessio-
nes. Omnīs autem illas Brutus vendiderat; et
tum, paterna emancupare praedia turpius habe-
batur. Similis in apologis quoque et quibusdam
interim etiam historiis exponendis gratia con-
sequi solet.)

[45] Sed acutior est illa, atque velocior in urbanitate, brevitas. Cuius quidem duplex forma
est, dicendi ac respondendi, sed ratio commu-
nis in parte; nihil enim quod in lacessendo dici
potest, non etiam in repercutiendo; at quaedam
propria sunt respondentium. [46] Illa parata

Crassus, had advocated the opposite of what he'd pleaded for in his speech on the Servilian Law. Crassus himself then summoned *three* readers, and he assigned them parts of the *Dialogues* written by Brutus's father to read. Since part 1 covered a conversation the two of them had while they were at an estate in Privernum, part 2 at one in Alba, and part 3 at one in Tivoli, Crassus kept asking where all those estates were—but Brutus had sold them all, and back then, people took a dim view of liquidating family properties. Similar smiles tend to result from telling Aesopic fables or even, if timed right, certain historical anecdotes.)

[45] But with wisecracks, brevity is quicker and punchier than that. It comes in two kinds, the quip and the comeback, but the thinking behind both is partly the same, since there isn't anything you can say as an attack that you can't also say as a retort. Comebacks, on the other hand, do have some special properties of their

atque cogitata afferri solent, haec plerùmque in
altercatione aut in rogandis testibus reperiuntur. Quom sint autem loci plures ex quibus
dicta ridicula ducantur, repetendum est mihi
non omnīs eos oratoribus convenire, [47] imprimis ex amphibolia, neque illa obscura quae
Atellanio more captant, nec qualia vulgò iactan-
tur a vilissimo quōque, conversā in maledictum
fere ambiguitate—ne illa quidem quae Ciceroni
aliquando (sed non in agendo) exciderunt; ut
dixit, quom is candidatus qui coqui filius habe-
batur coram eo suffragium ab alio peteret,

   "Ego 'quoque' tibi favebo!"

own. [46] Quips tend to arrive prepared and thought-through, whereas comebacks are generally discovered in the course of a debate or in questioning witnesses. Since there are lots and lots of observations you can use as a basis for funny wisecracks, though, it's incumbent on me to repeat that not all of them are suitable for orators, [47] least of all puns, either as riddles couched in captious improv style or the kind that tasteless people are constantly volleying back and forth, where the ambiguity is basically there to insult somebody. Unsuitable are even those that Cicero sometimes let slip (though not in court). For example, there was a candidate running for office whose father was believed to be a cook. When he went to ask a man for his vote, Cicero, who was standing by, piped up,

"Roast assured—*I*'ll support you!"[58]

[48]—non quia excludenda sint omnino verba duos sensūs significantia, sed quia rarò belle respondeant, nisi quom prorsus rebus ipsis adiuvantur. Quare, non hoc modò, sed paene ét ipsum scurrile est in eundem (de quo supra dixi) Isauricum:

"Miror quid sit quod pater tuus, homo constantissimus, te nobis 'varium' reliquit."

[49] Sed illud ex eodem genere praeclarum, quom obiceret Miloni accusator, in argumentum factarum Clodio insidiarum, quod Bovillas ante horam nonam devertisset ut expectaret dum Clodius a villā suā exiret, et identidem interrogaret quo tempore Clodius occisus esset, respondit,

"Sērò."

[48] I don't mean that words with two meanings should be banned altogether, it's just that they hardly ever fit the situation nicely, except when the actual facts support them completely. That's why not only was that example virtually stand-up, but so is the remark directed against Isauricus, who I mentioned earlier [*in section 25*]:

> "I just don't get how your father—a paragon of independence—could leave us someone as 'whipped' as you."[59]

[49] On the other hand, there *is* a really sterling example of that type. In order to prove he'd ambushed Clodius, the prosecutor alleged that Milo had stopped off at Bovillae to wait for Clodius to leave his villa, and before 3:00 p.m. When he then kept asking, over and over, "*When* was he killed?!?" Milo replied,

> "Late!"[60]

—quod vél solum sufficit ut hoc genus non totum repudietur.

[50] Nec plura modo significari solent, sed etiam diversa; ut Nero de servo pessimo dixit, nulli plus apud se fidei haberi:

"Nihil ei nec occlusum neque signatum esse."

[51] Pervenit res usque ad aenigma, quale est Ciceronis in Plaetorium Fontei accusatorem,

"Cuius matrem (*dixit*) dum vixisset 'ludum,' postquam mortua esset, 'magistros' habuisse."

Dicebantur autem, dum vixit, infames feminae convenire ad eam solitae; post mortem,

—and that, all by itself, is enough to keep us from rejecting this type categorically.

Types and Techniques of Wisecracks

[50] And it's not just more than one thing that some words can mean, but even their opposites.[61] For example [*borrowed from Cicero, section 248*], of a truly awful slave, Nero quipped,

"Nothing is sealed or off limits to him."

[51] The thing sometimes winds up a puzzle. An example is Cicero's swipe at Plaetorius, the accuser of Fonteius,

"In life, his mother had a *ludus* (school/brothel); in death, she had *magistri* (teachers/estate liquidators)."

That is, loose women allegedly used to gather at her house while she was alive, whereas her

bona eius vēnierant. (Quamquam hīc, "ludus" per tralationem dictum est, "magistri" per ambiguitatem.)

[52] In metalempsin quoque cadit eadem ratio dictorum; ut Fabius Maximus, incusans Augusti congiariorum quae amicis dabantur exiguitatem,

"Heminaria"

esse dixit, nam congiarium commune liberalitatis atque mensurae (a mensurā, ductā imminutione rerum). [53] Haec tám frigida quám est nominum fictio adiectis detractis mutatis litteris; ut

- Acisculum, quia esset pactus, "Paciscu-lum"; et
- Placidum nomine, quod is acerbus natura esset, "Acidum"; et

property was sold off upon her death. (Although, here *ludus* is a metaphor (a "school" of love), while *magistri* is a pun.)

[52] The same sort of joke also sometimes falls under "metalepsis." For example, underwhelmed with the "gifts" [*congiaria*] the Emperor Augustus was giving his friends, Fabius Maximus quipped,

"They're teaspoons!"

—because *congiarium* means both a gift and a gallon, and he used the unit of measure to disparage the things. [53] That's as weak as making up names by adding, subtracting, or changing letters; examples I've found include calling:

- Acisculum, because it was *paci*fied, "Paci"sculum;
- Placidus, because he had a *scathing* personality, "Acid"us; and

- Tullium, quom fur esset, "Tollium"
  dictos invenio.

[54] Sed haec eadem genera commodius
in rebus quàm in nominibus respondent. Afer
enim venuste Manlium Suram multum in agendo
discursantem salientem, manūs iactantem, togam
deicientem et reponentem,

"non agere (*dixit*) sed 'satagere.'"

Est enim dictum per se urbanum "satagere,"
etiam si nulla subsit alterius verbi similitudo.

[55] Fiunt ét adiectā ét detractā adspiratione
et divisis coniunctisque verbis similiter, saepius
frigida, aliquando tamen recipienda: eademque
condicio est in iis quae a nominibus trahuntur.
Multa ex hōc genere Cicero "In Verrem," sed ut

- Tullius, because he was a *thief*, "Steal"ius.

[54] But these gimmicks work better with things than names. You see, when Manlius Sura was acting as lead attorney in a case and kept running and jumping around, throwing his hands up, and fumbling with his toga, Afer quipped,

"He's not 'acting': he's acting up!"

You see, "acting up" is an inherently funny phrase, and it would be even if it didn't resemble the other word.

[55] Most of the time, adding or subtracting the letter *h* and dividing and joining words is just as weak, though sometimes it's acceptable, and it's the same story with jokes based on names. Cicero has a lot of those in his speech

ab aliis dicta:

- modo futurum ut omnia "verreret,"
- modo Herculi, quem expilaverat, molestiorem quàm "aprum Erymanthium" fuisse,
- modo "malum sacerdotem" qui tam nequam "verrem" reliquisset (quia Sacerdoti Verres successerat).

[56] Praebet tamen aliquando occasionem quaedam felicitas hōc quoque bene utendi; ut "Pro Caecina" Cicero in testem Sex. Clodium Phormionem,

"Nec minus niger (*inquit*) nec minus confidens quàm est ille Terentianus 'Phormio.'"

attacking Verres—whose name means "boar"—
though they're always attributed to others:

- "He's going to 'sweep' [*verrere*] everything away."
- "He was tougher on his victim than the
  Erymanthian boar was on Hercules."
- "It was a bad 'priest' who left such a
  worthless boar/Verres behind." (Verres's
  predecessor was a man named Priest.)

[56] Every now and then, though, a little luck
does give us a chance to make good use of this
trick. An example is Cicero's attack in his speech
In Defense of Caecina [27] on a witness named
Sextus Clodius Phormio [*who was a banker*]:

"He's just as 'shady' and nervy a character as that Phormio in Terence's play."[62]

[57] Acriora igitur sunt et elegantiora quae trahuntur ex vi rerum. In iis maxime valet similitudo, si tamen ad aliquid inferius leviusque re-
feratur; qualia veteres illi iocabantur, qui
Lentulum "Spintherem" et Scipionem "Serap-
ionem" esse dixerunt. Sed ea non ab hominibus
modo petitur, verùm etiam ab animalibus; ut
nobis pueris Iunius Bassus, homo imprimis
dicax, [58] "Asinus albus" vocabatur, et Sarmentus Messium Cicirrum "equo fero" similem
dixit; et ab inanimis, ut P. Blessius Iulium, hominem nigrum et macrum et pandum, "fibulam
ferream" dixit. Quod nunc risūs petendi genus
frequentissimum est.

[59] Adhibetur autem similitudo interim
palam, interim more parabolae; cuius est ge-

[57] Accordingly, jokes based on the meaning of things are punchier and more sophisticated. Resemblance is the most important element in them, provided the point of reference is something humbler and less consequential, like the jokes our ancestors made in nicknaming Lentulus "Spinther" and Scipio "Serapio."[63] And you can look for resemblances not only from people, but from animals, too. For example, when I was a kid people used to call Junius Bassus—who was a *serious* jerk—a [58] "white jackass," while Sarmentus said Messius Cicirrus was "like a wild horse." Inanimate objects can also be used. For example, Julius was a swarthy, skinny guy with slouching, rounded shoulders. Publius Blessius called him an "iron carabiner." And nowadays, this is an extremely common technique of trying to get a laugh.

[59] Sometimes resemblances are stated plainly and sometimes as absurd exaggerations. An example is the Emperor Augustus's classic.

neris illud Augusti, qui, militi libellum timide porrigenti,

"Noli (*inquit*) tamquam assem elephanto des."

[60] Sunt quaedam vi similia, unde Vatinius dixit hoc dictum quom reus, agente in eum Calvo, frontem candido sudario tergeret, idque ipsum accusator in invidiam vocaret,

"Quamvis reus sum (*inquit*), ét panem, tamen, candidum edo."

[61] Adhuc est subtilior illa ex simili tralatio, quom quod in aliā re fieri solet in aliam mutuamur;

When a soldier kept hesitantly handing him a petition, he quipped,

> "Come on, you're not feeding a peanut to an elephant."

[60] Some resemblances are based on an inner quality, which explains this quip by Vatinius. While denouncing him in court, Calvus tried to exploit the fact that Vatinius kept mopping his forehead with a *white* handkerchief [*rather than dark, since defendants traditionally wore dark clothing to court*]. Vatinius retorted,

> "Yes, you're blackening my name, but guess what: the bread I eat is still white, too."

[61] Even nicer than that is playing off a parallel, where we borrow the surrounding situation for our thing that typically belongs to another

ea dicatur sane "fictio"; ut Chrysippus, quom
in triumpho Caesaris eborea oppida essent tra-
lata et, post dies paucos, Fabi Maximi lignea,

"Thecas esse oppidorum Caesaris."

dixit. Et Pedo de retiario qui myrmillonem con-
sequebatur nec feriebat,

"Vivum (*inquit*) capere vult."

[62] Iungitur amphiboliae similitudo; ut a
Gabba, qui pilam neglegenter petenti,

"Sic (*inquit*) petis tamquam Caesaris
candidatus."

(you could of course call it "casting"). For example, Caesar's triumphal parade featured model towns made of ivory. A few days later, Fabius Maximus's triumph had wooden ones. Seeing them, Chrysippus quipped,

"There go the boxes Caesar's came in!"

Another: seeing one gladiator catch another in his net but refuse to finish him off, Pedo quipped,

"He wants to take him alive."

[62] Resemblances can be combined with puns. For example, a guy playing soccer wasn't really into the game. Gabba quipped,

"You're running about as hard as the Emperor's candidates do for election!"

Nam illud "petis" ambiguum est, securitas similis. Quod hactenus ostendisse, satis est.

[63] Ceterùm frequentissima aliorum generum cum aliis mixtura est, eaque optima quae ex pluribus constat. Eadem dissimilium ratio est. Hinc eques Romanus, ad quem in spectaculis bibentem quom misisset Augustus qui ei diceret, "Ego si prandere volo, domum eo,"

"Tu enim (*inquit*) non times ne locum perdas."

[64] Ex contrario, non una species. Neque enim eódem modo dixit (*1*) Augustus praefecto quem ignominiā mittebat, subinde interponenti precibus, "Quid respondebo patri meo?!":

You see, "running" is a pun, while the lack of effort is the resemblance. And that should be enough to make my point.

[63] All that said, the combination of some types with others is extremely common, the best of all being one with lots of them. The idea behind mismatches is the same. For example, Augustus spotted an upper middle-class Roman man drinking in the middle of a show. He sent a message over saying, "When I want to eat lunch, I go home." The man retorted,

"I bet! *You* don't need to worry about losing your seat."

[64] Opposites come in more than one kind. You see, it wasn't in the same way that (*1*) Augustus answered the officer he was giving a dishonorable discharge to, and who kept blubbering, "What am I going to tell my father?" Augustus answered,

"Dic me tibi displicuisse."

quó (2) Gabba paenulam roganti,

"Non possum commodare: domi maneo,"

quom cenaculum eius perplueret. (3) Tertium adhuc illud, nisi quod ut ne auctorem ponam, verecundia ipsius facit:

"Libidinosior es quàm ullus spado,"

quo, sine dubio, ét opinio decipitur, sed ex contrario.

Et hoc ex eodem loco est, sed nulli priorum simile, quod dixit M. Vestinus quom ei nuntiatum esset [. . . *some words missing* . . .],

"Aliquando desinet putere."

"Tell him I wasn't up to your standards."

—and that (2) Gabba replied to a man who asked to borrow his umbrella,

"I can't, sorry; I'm staying home,"

—since his dining room ceiling was leaking. And here's (3) a third, though I won't say who said it out of respect for the author:

"You're about as oversexed as a eunuch."

—which does take us by surprise, of course, but is also an example of an opposite.

And this next one is from this same category, but it's different from the previous examples. Marcus Vestinus said it when he heard [*that someone with awful body odor had died*]:

"Finally! He won't smell anymore."

[65] Onerabo librum exemplis, similemque iis qui risūs gratiā componuntur efficiam, si persequi voluero singula veterum.

Ex omnibus Argumentorum locis, eadem occasio est. Nam ét (*1*) Finitione usus est Augustus de pantomimis duobus qui alternis gestibus contendebant, quom eorum alterum "saltatorem" dixit, [66] alterum "interpellatorem," ét (*2*) Partitione Gabba, quom paenulam roganti respondit,

"Non pluit, non opus est tibi; si pluet, ipse utar."

Proinde, Genere Specie Propriis Differentibus Iugatis Adiunctis Consequentibus Antecedentibus Repugnantibus Causis Effectis, comparatione parium maiorum minorum similis materia praebetur,

[65] But I'm going to overload this discussion and turn it into a straight-out joke book if I include every last example the ancients left us.[64]

Further Types and Techniques of Wisecracks, and Their Relation to Rhetorical Figures

Every Line of Argument offers an opportunity for a witticism.[65] Thus, Augustus used (*1*) Definition for two street dancers that were miming gestures back and forth. He called one of them "the lead," and the other [66] "the interrupter." Gabba used (*2*) Partition when he told the man asking to borrow his umbrella,

> "It's not raining, so you don't need it; if it does rain, I'll use it myself."

They all work this way, in category after category.

sicut in Tropos quoque omnīs cadit. [67] An non plurima dicuntur (*1*) per Hyperbolen ridicula? Ut quod refert Cicero de homine praelongo,

"Caput eum ad fornicem Fabium offendisse,"

et quod P. Oppius dixit de genere Lentulorum, quom assidue minores parentibus liberi essent,

"Nascendo interiturum."

[68] (*2*) Quid Ironia? Nonne etiam quae severissime fit, ioci paene genus est? Qua urbane usus est Afer, quom Didio Gallo, qui provinciam ambitiosissime petierat, deinde—impetratā eā—

It's the same with the Figures of Speech, too. [67] Aren't a huge number of jokes (*1*) Hyperbole? An example is Cicero's quip [*in 267*] about a really tall guy:

> "He bumped his head on a triumphal arch."

Another is Publius Oppius's quip about the Lentulus family, where the children kept getting progressively shorter than their parents:

> "Birth's gonna be the cause of their extinction."

[68] (*2*) What about Irony? Even at its harshest, isn't it basically a kind of joke? Gallus maneuvered like crazy to get himself assigned [*the lucrative job of administering*] a province, and, once he got it, he kept acting like he'd been

tamquam "coactus" querebatur:

"Age (*inquit*), ¡aliquid ét rei publicae causā!"

(*3*) Metaphorā quoque Cicero lusit, quom Vatini morte nuntiatā, cuius parum certus dicebatur auctor,

"Interim (*inquit*) usurā fruar."

[69] (*4*) Idem per Allegorian M. Caelium, melius obicientem crimina quàm defendentem,

"Bonam dextram, malam sinistram habere."

dicebat. (*5*) Emphasi A. Villius dixit

forced to take it. Afer then made clever use of irony, quipping,

"Come on, do something for your country, too."

(3) Cicero also used Metaphor to make a joke. When he heard of Vatinius's death but wasn't sure of the reliability of the rumor, he quipped,

"If I can't buy it, I'll take the loan."

[69] (4) He also used Allegory in saying of Marcus Caelius, who was better at pressing charges than refuting them,

"He's got a good right hook, but his left is weak."

(5) Aulus Villius used Suggestive Language in saying,

"Ferrum in Tuccium incidisse."

[70] Figuras quoque Mentis, quae "σχήματα διανοίας" dicuntur, res eadem recipit omnīs, in quas nonnulli diviserunt species dictorum. Nam ét Interrogamus ét Dubitamus ét Affirmamus ét Minamur ét Optamus; quaedam ut miserantes, quaedam ut irascentes dicimus. Ridiculum est autem omne quod aperte fingitur.

[71] Stulta reprehendere facillimum est (nam per se sunt ridicula), sed rem urbanam facit aliqua ex nobis adiectio. Stulte interrogaverat exeuntem de theatro Campatium Titius Maximus an spectasset. Fecit Campatius dubitationem eius stultiorem dicendo,

"Non, sed in orchestra pilā lusi."

[72] Refutatio quom sit in (*1*) Negando (*2*) Redarguendo (*3*) Defendendo (*4*) Elevando

"Tuccius got engraved by a sword."[66]

[70] The same goes for all the Figures of Thought—the *schemata dianoias*—which some use to classify jokes. You see, we Wonder about, Ask Questions about, Agree with, Threaten, Wish, and Sympathize or Get Angry about some of the things we say. Conducted aloud, all such thinking is funny.

[71] Criticizing stupidity is easy because stupidity is funny all by itself, but a little fillip from us makes it witty. Campatius was filing out of a theater and Maximus asked him, stupidly, if he'd seen the show. Campatius's reply made Maximus's question look even stupider:

"No, I was playing soccer onstage."

[72] Refutation works by (*1*) Denying, (*2*) Rebutting, (*3*) Justifying, (*4*) Mitigating, and

(*5*) Transferendo, (*1*) ridicule negavit Q. Curius; nam quom eius accusator in sipario omnibus locis aut nudum eum in nervo aut ab amicis redemptum ex aleā pinxisset,

"Ergo ego (*inquit*) *numquam* vici!?"

[73] (*2*) Redarguimus (*2.a*) interim aperte; ut Cicero Vibium Curium multum de annis aetatis suae mentientem,

"Tum ergo quom unā declamabamus non eras natus,"

(*2.b*) interim ét simulatā adsensione, ut īdem Fabiā Dolabellae dicente triginta se annos habere,

(5) Shifting. A funny example of (*1*) is the denial of Quintus Curius. The prosecution made a visual presentation for the judges of him in which, in every image, he was either sitting naked in the public stocks or getting bailed out at the poker table by his friends. He quipped,

"Sheesh, didn't I ever win?"

[73] (*2*) We can rebut (*2.a*) openly. For example, when Vibius Curius kept lying about his age, Cicero quipped,

"Ah, I see; I guess you and I were practicing together before you were born."

Or (*2.b*) we can rebut by pretending we're in agreement. For example, when Dolabella's wife claimed to be 30 years old, Cicero quipped,

"Verum est (*inquit*)! Nam hoc illam iam viginti annis audio."

[74] Belle interim subicitur pro eo quod neges, aliud mordacius; ut Iunius Bassus, querente Domitiā Passieni quod—incusans eius sordes—calceos eam veteres diceret vendere solere,

"Non mehercules (*inquit*) hoc umquam dixi, sed dixi 'emere' te solere."

(*3*) Defensionem imitatus est eques Romanus qui, obicienti Augusto quod patrimonium comedisset,

"Meum (*inquit*) putavi."

[75] (*4*) Elevandi ratio est duplex, (*4.a*) ut aut vanam quis iactantiam minuat, quemadmodum

"It's true! I've been hearing her say it for 20 years now."[67]

[74] It's sometimes nice to replace the thing you deny with something that stings worse. For example, Junius Bassus called Domitia a cheapskate, saying she routinely sold her old shoes. When she got upset, he quipped,

"Lord no! I never said that; I said you *buy* 'em."

(3) An upper-middle-class guy produced a model justification. He blew through his inheritance, and when the Emperor reprimanded him, he quipped,

"I thought it was mine."

[75] (4) Mitigation takes two forms: (4.a) Cutting idiotic nonsense down to size, as Caesar

C. Caesar Pomponio ostendenti vulnus ore exceptum in seditione Sulpicianā, quod is se "passum pro Caesare pugnantem" gloriabatur,

"Numquam fugiens respexeris (*inquit*),"

(*4.b*) aut crimen obiectum; ut Cicero obiurgantibus quod sexagenarius Publiliam virginem duxisset,

"Cras mulier erit (*inquit*)."

[76] Hoc genus dicti "Consequens" vocant quidam, estque illi simile quod Cicero Curionem, semper ab excusatione aetatis incipientem,

[*the main speaker in Cicero's dialogue*] did to Pomponius. Pomponius was showing off a facial wound he'd received in Sulpicius's uprising, and he kept boasting he'd gotten it fighting for Caesar. Caesar replied,

"You should *never* look back when running away."

(*4.b*) Alternatively, cutting down the charge. For example, when people criticized Cicero, who was in his sixties, for marrying a teenage virgin girl, he replied,

"She'll be a woman tomorrow."

[76] Some people call this kind of a joke a "Consequence." Akin to it is what Cicero said about Curio, who always began his speeches by apologizing for his youth.

"Facilius cotidie prooemium habere,"

dixit, quia ista naturā sequi et cohaerere videantur. [77] Sed Elevandi genus est etiam Causarum
Relatio, qua Cicero est usus in Vatinium. Qui
pedibus aeger quom vellet videri commodioris
valetudinis factus et diceret se iam bina milia
passuum ambulare,

"Dies enim (*inquit*) longiores sunt."

Et Augustus, nuntiantibus Terraconensibus
palmam in arā eius enatam,

"Apparet (*inquit*) quàm saepe accendatis."

[78] (5) Transtulit crimen Cassius Severus; nam
quom obiurgaretur a praetore quod advocati

"That part gets easier for him every day."

It gets its name because the two parts seem to follow and link up automatically. [77] Attributing Reasons is also a kind of Mitigation; Cicero used it on Vatinius. Vatinius had trouble walking, and when he wanted to look as though he were getting better, he claimed he was going for a 2-mile walk every day. Cicero quipped,

"Yes, the days *are* getting longer . . ."

And when the people of Tarraco reported that a palm tree had sprouted upon the incense altar dedicated to him, Augustus quipped,

"Shows how often you light it!"

[78] (5) Shifting a Charge is illustrated by Cassius Severus. When a judge was blasting him

eius L. Vario Epicureo, Caesaris amico, convicium fecissent,

"Nescio (*inquit*) qui conviciati sint . . . et puto Stoicos fuisse."

Repercutiendi multa sunt genera, venustissimum quod etiam similitudine aliquā verbi adiuvatur; ut Trachalus dicenti Suillio, "Si hoc ita est, is in exilium,"

"Si non est ita, redis (*inquit*)."

[79] Elusit Cassius Severus, obiciente quodam quod ei domo suā Proculeius interdixisset, respondendo,

"Numquid ego illuc accedo?"

because his lawyer had insulted an Epicurean friend of Augustus, he replied,

> "I have no *idea* who insulted him, and I'm pretty sure he's a Stoic."[68]

There are many types of retorts, the most charming being one that's helped by some verbal similarity. For example, Trachalus told Suillius, "If this is true, you're going to prison." He replied,

> "If it's not true, you're going back [*to prison*]."[69]

[79] Evasion is illustrated by Cassius Severus. A man taunted Severus because he got slapped with an order prohibiting him from entering the man's house. Severus replied,

> "Do I ever go?"

225

Sed eluditur ét ridiculum ridiculo—ut divus
Augustus, quom ei Galli torquem aureum cen-
tum pondo dedissent et Dolabella, per iocum
(temptans tamen ioci sui eventum) dixisset,
"Imperator, torque me donā!"

"Mālo (*inquit*) te civicā donare."

[80]—mendacium quoque mendacio; ut Gabba,
dicente quodam victoriato se uno in Sicilia
quinque pedes longam murenam emisse,

"Nihil (*inquit*) mirum; nam ibi tam lon-
gae nascuntur ut iis piscatores pro resti-
bus cingantur."

[81] Contraria est Neganti confessionis simulatio, sed ipsa quoque multum habet urbanitatis.

You can also evade a joke with a joke. For example, the Gauls made a gift of a 100-pound gold necklace to the divine Augustus. Half-joking—and half not—Dolabella said, "General! Present *me* with that necklace!" Augustus replied,

> "I'd rather present you with the Civic Crown" [*a supreme but token honor*].

[80] And you can evade a lie with a lie. For example, a man claimed to have bought a 5-foot-long eel in Sicily for a buck. Gabba quipped,

> "I'm not surprised! They get so big down there it's the eels, not the ropes, that the fishermen get tangled up in."

[81] Pretending to Confess is the opposite of Denial, but it too can be very witty. For example,

Sic Afer, quom ageret contra libertum Claudi Caesaris et ex diverso quidam condicionis eiusdem cuius erat litigator exclamasset, "Praeterea, ¡tu semper in libertos Caesaris dicis!"

"Nec mehercule (*inquit*) quicquam proficio."

Cui vicinum est non negare quod obicitur, quom ét id palam falsum est ét inde materia bene respondendi datur; ut Catulus, dicenti Philippo, "Quid latras?"

"Furem video (*inquit*)."

[82] In se dicere non fere est nisi scurrarum et in oratore utique, minime probabile; quod fieri totidem modis quot in alios potest, ideoque hoc,

Afer was pleading a case against one of the Emperor's freedmen. All of a sudden, a man from the same social class on the other side shouted, "Yeah, you're always attacking the Emperor's freedmen!" "Goddamn right," quipped Afer,

"... and it never gets me anywhere!"

Close to this is *not* denying a charge when it's obviously false and when it offers material for a good comeback. For example, when Philippus asked Barker [*in Cicero, section 220*], "What are you howling for?" he replied,

"I see a thief."

[82] Making a joke at your own expense is really something only stand-up comedians do, and at any rate it's not at all appropriate for an orator. You can do it in as many ways as you can do it

quamvis frequens sit, transeo.

[83] Illud verò, etiam si ridiculum est, indignum tamen est homine liberali, quod aut turpiter aut petulanter dicitur; quod fecisse quendam scio qui humiliori libere adversùs se loquenti,

"Colaphum (*inquit*) tibi ducam—et formulam scribam, 'quod caput durum habeas.'"

Hīc enim dubium est utrum ridere audientes an indignari debuerint.

[84] Superest genus (*1*) decipiendi opinionem aut (*2*) dicta aliter intellegendi, quae sunt in omni hac materiā vél venustissima.

to others, and hence, common though it is, I pass it over.

[83] By contrast, a bullying or terrorizing remark is unworthy of a decent person, even if it's funny. I know someone who did this. When a lower-status man kept on attacking him in a debate, he said,

> "I'm about to punch you in the face and then sue you for having such a thick skull."

The problem here is deciding whether the audience should have laughed or cried out in protest.

Remaining Types of Wisecracks

[84] There remain the categories of (1) fooling expectations and (2) misunderstanding words, which are far and away the funniest and most charming in this area.

(*1*) Inopinatum ét (*1.a*) a lacessente poni solet, quale est quod refert Cicero,

"¿Quid huic abest—nisi res et virtus?"

aut illud Afri,

"Homo in agendis causis optime vestitus;"

ét (*1.b*) in occurrendo; ut Cicero, auditā falsā Vatini morte, quom obvium libertum eius interrogasset "Rectene omnia?" dicenti "Recte,"

"Mortuus est (*inquit*)."

[85] (*2*) Plurimus autem circa (*2.a*) Simulationem et (*2.b*) Dissimulationem risus est, quae sunt

(*1*) Surprises tend to be used both by (*1.a*) the challenger, such as Cicero's [*section 281*]

"That guy has it all—except money and redeeming qualities."

or Afer's remark about some fancypants,

"For pleading cases, that guy's *perfectly* 'suited.'"

and (*1.b*) in comebacks for example, Cicero heard a false rumor of Vatinius's death; he then ran into one of Vatinius's freedmen and asked, "All good?" "All good," said the man, to which Cicero replied,

"He *is* dead!"

[85] (*2*) The most laughs, though, cluster around (*2.a*) Faking It and (*2.b*) Playing Innocent.

vicina et prope eadem, sed Simulatio est certam opinionem animi sui imitantis, Dissimulatio aliena se parum intellegere fingentis.

(*2.a*) Simulavit Afer quom, in causā subinde dicentibus "Celsinam" de re cognovisse (quae erat potens femina),

"Quis est (*inquit*) iste?"

Celsinam enim videri sibi virum finxit.

[86] (*2.b*) Dissimulavit Cicero quom Sex. Annalis testis reum laesisset et instaret identidem accusator, "Dic, M. Tulli, si quid potes de Sexto Annali"; versūs enim dicere coepit de libro

They're neighbors, almost twins even, but Faking It amounts to imitating your heart's true opinion, while Playing Innocent amounts to pretending you don't understand someone else's words.

(*2.a*) Faking It is illustrated by Afer's remark in a dispute in which person after person kept saying that Celsina (an influential lady) had decided the case:

"Who's he?"

inquired Afer. (He acted as if he thought Celsina was a man's name.)

[86] (*2.b*) Playing Innocent is illustrated by Cicero's remark. A witness named Sixtus Annalis had damaged Cicero's client, and the prosecutor kept pressing the point over and over: "Tell us, Cicero, what can you say—if anything—of Sixtus Annalis?" Whereupon Cicero

Enni "Annali" sexto:

> ♫"Quis potis ingentis causas evolvere
> belli?"♫

[87] Cui sine dubio frequentissimam dat occasionem ambiguitas; ut Cascellio, qui consultatori dicenti, "Navem dividere volo,"

"Perdes (*inquit*)."

Sed averti intellectus ét aliter solet, quom ab asperioribus ad leniora deflectitur; ut qui, interrogatus quid sentiret de eo qui in adulterio deprehensus esset,

"Tardum fuisse"

began to quote lines from the sixth book of Ennius's *Annals*:

♪" Who could ever disclose the reasons
for breathtaking warfare . . . ?"♪

[87] Ambiguity surely provides the most frequent opportunities for this. It did for Cascellius. When a client ⌈*getting divorced*⌉ told him, "I want to split the boat," he quipped,

"You'll lose." / "You'll ruin it."[70]

Meaning often tends to get twisted in another way, when it gets redirected from something harsher to something softer. For example, a man was asked his opinion of a guy caught *in flagrante delicto*.

"Should've moved faster,"

respondit. [88] Ei confine est quod dicitur per suspicionem, quale illud apud Ciceronem querenti quod uxor sua ex fico se suspendisset,

"Rogo des mihi surculum ex illā arbore ut inseram."

Intellegitur enim quod non dicitur.

[89] Ét, hercule, *omnis* salse dicendi ratio in eo est, ut aliter quàm est rectum verumque dicatur; quod fit totum (*1*) fingendis aut (*1.a*) nostris aut (*1.b*) alienis persuasionibus, aut (*2*) dicendo quod fieri non potest.

[90] (*1.b*) Alienam finxit Iuba, qui, querenti quod "ab equo" suo esset adspersus,

he answered. [88] Bordering this are loaded remarks. An example is the reply in Cicero [*section 278*] to a man wailing that his wife had hung herself from a fig tree:

"Any chance I could get a cutting from that tree for a grafting?"

The implication of that one is clear.

The Theoretical Basis of Humor in General, with Sterling Examples

[89] Indeed, the whole idea behind humor lies in saying something in a different, wrong, and untrue way. It comes wholly from (*1*) inventing beliefs—either (*1.a*) our own or (*1.b*) other people's—or (*2*) from saying something impossible.

[90] Juba demonstrated (*1.b*) inventing other people's beliefs. A man complained of getting spattered by Juba's horse. "Huh?" asked Juba,

"Quid, ¿tu (*inquit*) me Hippocentaurum putas?"

(*1.a*) Suam C. Cassius, qui, militi sine gladio decurrenti,

"Heus, commilito, ¡pugno bene utĕris! (*inquit*),"

et Gabba de piscibus qui, quom prídie ex parte adesi et versati, póstero die positi essent,

"Festinemus—alii subcenant (*inquit*)."

(*2*) Tertium illud Cicero, ut dixi, adversùs Curium; fieri enim certe non poterat ut quom declamaret natus non esset. [91] Est ét illa ex

"What am I, a centaur?"

Gaius Cassius demonstrated (*1.a*) inventing his own. A soldier was doing drills without his sword. "Man," he quipped,

"You're great with that fist!"

So did Gabba, when there were these half-eaten fish left over from the day before. The next day, they were served to him flipped over, with the uneaten side up. He quipped,

"Quick, let's eat! Others have already started!"[71]

Cicero demonstrated the third [*i.e., 2*] in the swipe at Curius that I quoted earlier [*section 72*]. I mean, it was obviously impossible for him to have not been born when he was practicing. [91] There's also invention based on irony,

ironia fictio, qua usus est C. Caesar. Nam quom testis diceret a reo fĕmina sua ferro petita, et esset facilis reprehensio, cur illam potissimum partem corporis vulnerare voluisset,

"¿Quid enim faceret (*inquit*), quom tu galeam et loricam haberes?"

[92] Vél optima est autem simulatio contra simulantem, qualis illa Domiti Afri fuit. Vetus habebat testamentum, et unus ex amicis recentioribus, sperans aliquid ex mutatione tabularum, falsam fabulam intulerat, consulens eum ¿an primipilari seni—iam testato—suaderet ordinare suprema iudicia:

which Caesar [*probably the speaker in Cicero*] made use of. A witness claimed that a defendant had taken stabs at his thighs with a sword. Rebutting him would have been easy; he could've asked why the man had wanted to wound *that* particular part of the body. Instead Caesar quipped,

"Give me a break! You had a helmet and breastplate!"

[92] The absolute best, however, is hoisting a faker by his own petard. Domitius Afer once demonstrated it. He had drawn up his will long ago, and one of his newer friends hoped to finagle something by getting him to reassign his bequests. He concocted a story and went to ask Afer's advice: "There's this elderly officer. . . . He's already drawn up his will, but . . . should I have him arrange for his last and final wishes?" "Don't," replied Afer,

"Noli (*inquit*) facere; offendis illum."

[93] Iucundissima sunt autem ex his omnibus lenta et, ut sic dixerim, boni stomachi; ut Afer īdem ingrato litigatori conspectum eius in Foro vitanti per nomenclatorem missum ad eum,

"Amas me (*inquit*), quod te non vidi?"

et dispensatori qui, quom reliqua non reponeret, dicebat subinde, "Non comedi! Pane et aquā vivo!"

"Passer, redde quod debes."

—quae "ὑπὸ τὸ ἦθος" vocant.

244

"You're offending him."

[93] Out of all these types, though, the most fun are good-humored, not dyspeptic jokes (so to speak). More examples from Afer: An ungrateful client was avoiding him in the Forum. Afer sent his assistant over to say,

"I hope you appreciate me not noticing you."

He had a steward, too, who didn't come back with the change from purchases and would repeat, "I didn't party it away—I'm the bread-and-water type!" Afer quipped,

"OK, sparrow! Pay back what you owe."

In Greek they call that kind of thing *hypo to ethos* ["getting at character"].[72]

[94] Est gratus iocus qui minus exprobrat quàm potest; ut īdem dicenti candidato, "Semper domum tuam colui," quom posset palam negare,

"Credo (*inquit*), ut verum."

Interim, de se dicere ridiculum est; et, quod in alium si absentem diceretur urbanum non erat, quoniam ipsi palam exprobratur, movet risum; [95] quale Augusti est, quom ab eo miles nescioquid improbe peteret et veniret contra Marcianus, quem suspicabatur et ipsum aliquid iniuste rogaturum,

"Non magis (*inquit*) faciam, commilito, quod petis quàm quod Marcianus a me petiturus est."

[94] A nice joke is one that criticizes less than it could. For example, a man running for office told Afer, "I've always cherished your family." Afer could have simply denied it, but he quipped,

"I believe it—just like the truth."[73]

Speaking about ourselves is sometimes funny, and a remark that would be tasteless behind a person's back can raise a laugh when it roasts the person publicly. [95] For example, a soldier was in the middle of making some improper request of Augustus when up came a bigwig who, Augustus assumed, was also about to ask for some special favor. "Sir," quipped Augustus,

"I'll no more grant your request than whatever this big shot's about to hit me up for."

[96] Adiuvant urbanitatem ét versūs commode positi, seú (*1*) toti ut sunt (quod adeo facile est ut Ovidius ex "Tetrastichōn" Macri "carmine" librum in malos poetas composuerit), quod fit gratius si qua etiam ambiguitate conditur; ut Cicero in Lartium, hominem callidum et versutum, quom is in quadam causā suspectus esset,

♫"Nisi si quā Ulixes lintre evasit
    Lartius,"♫

[97] seú (*2*) verbis ex parte mutatis; ut in eum qui, quom antea stultissimus esset habitus,

ON THE ART OF HUMOR

*The Art of Riffing on Famous Lines
and Lyrics*

[96] Sophisticated wit is amplified by the apt quotation of poetry, either (*1*) wholesale and verbatim (which is so easy that Ovid wrote a book attacking bad poets by quoting Macer's quatrains), which gets even better if it's—(*heh, heh*) "built"—with a little ambiguity.[74] An example is Cicero's swipe at Lartius, a crafty and complicated man, when he was a suspect in some case:

> ♩ ". . . unless he had the raft
> Odysseus Lartius used to make his
> getaway."[75] ♩

[97] Or alternatively, (*2*) by changing the words somewhat. An example is the swipe at a senator who'd always been regarded as a total idiot;

post acceptam hereditatem primus sententiam rogabatur,

♫"Hereditas est quam vocant
　　'sapientiam,'"♫

pro illo "felicitas est"; seú (3) ficti, notis versibus similes, quae "παρῳδία" dicitur; [98] et proverbia oportune aptata; ut homini nequam lapso et ut adlevaretur roganti,

"Tollat te qui non novit."

Ex historiā etiam ducere urbanitatem eruditum est; ut Cicero fecit quom ei testem in iudicio Verris roganti dixisset Hortensius, "Non intellego haec aenigmata,"

after receiving his inheritance, he started being asked to weigh in on matters first:

♫"Inheritance is but a name for
  wisdom."♫

"Inheritance" has replaced "Happiness." Alternatively, (3) you can make up lines of poetry that resemble famous ones (this is called "parody" in Greek). [98] Turning proverbs into zingers is effective, too. Say, for example, a mean guy falls down. When he asks for help getting up, you could say,

"Allow the stranger to lift you up."

It's also a sign of good education to draw on history for a witticism. For example, when Cicero called a witness at Verres's trial, Hortensius told him, "I'm baffled by this riddle." "Well, you shouldn't be," quipped Cicero,

"Atqui debes (*inquit*), quom Sphingem domi habeas."

(Acceperat autem ille a Verre Sphingem aeneam magnae pecuniae.)

[99] Subabsurda illa constant stulti simulatione; quae nisi fingantur, stulta sunt; ut qui mirantibus quod humile candelabrum emisset,

"Pransorium erit (*inquit*)."

Sed illa similia absurdis sunt acria quae tamquam sine ratione dicta feruntur; ut servus Dolabellae, quom interrogaretur an dominus eius auctionem proposuisset,

"Domum (*inquit*) vendidit."

"You have a sphinx at home."

(Hortensius had received an expensive bronze sphinx from Verres.[76])

The Art of Deadpan

[99] "Non sequiturs" consist of feigning stupidity. (If it's *not* a pretense, then they really are stupid.) For example, a man bought a miniature candlestick. When people asked why, he replied,

"It's to use at brunch."

Sometimes a seemingly illogical remark that looks like a non sequitur is actually a shiv. For example, one of Dolabella's slaves was asked, "Did your master advertise a yard sale?" He replied,

"He sold the house."[77]

[100] Deprensi interim pudorem suum ridiculo aliquo explicant; ut qui testem dicentem se a reo vulneratum interrogaverat an cicatricem haberet, quom ille ingentem in fĕmine ostendisset,

"Latus (*inquit*) oportuit."

Contumeliis quoque uti belle datur; ut Hispo, obicienti atrociora crimina accusatori,

"Me ex te metiris? (*inquit*)."

Et Fulvius Propinquus legato interroganti an in tabulis quas proferebat chirographus esset,

"Et verus (*inquit*), domine."

[100] People who get caught out sometimes tell a joke to save face. For example, a witness was claiming a defendant had stabbed him. "Do you have a scar?" the lawyer asked. When the witness revealed a huge one on his thigh, the lawyer replied,

"I meant on your side."[78]

Insults are another nice possibility. For example, when a man charged Hispo with heinous crimes, he asked,

"Are you holding *me* to *your* standards?"

Likewise, a lieutenant asked Fulvius Propinquus, "Is there a signature on that order you've brought?" "Yessir," he replied,

"—and real, too."

[101] Has aut accepi species aut inveni fre-
quentissimas ex quibus ridicula ducerentur, sed
repetam necesse est infinitas esse tám salse dicendi quám severe, quas praestat persona locus
tempus, casus denique, qui est maxime varius.
[102] Itaque, haec ne omisisse viderer attigi; illa
autem, quae de usu ipso et modo iocandi complexus sum, affirmarim esse plane necessaria.

His adicit Domitius Marsus, qui "De Urbanitate" diligentissime scripsit, quaedam non
ridicula, sed cuilibet severissimae orationi con-
venientia eleganter dicta et proprio quodam
lepore iucunda; quae sunt quidem urbana, sed
risum tamen non habent. [103] Neque enim ei

[101] That covers all the categories I've learned or identified as the most common sources of jokes, but I must reiterate that they're as infinite for humor as they are for speaking in earnest. They're a function of person, time, place, and not least luck, which is subject to big swings. [102] Accordingly, I've given them fairly short shrift (I didn't want to look like I was skipping them entirely). My earlier and more detailed remarks, though—about the actual use and manner of joking—those I do not hesitate to call clearly essential.[79]

An Appendix on Urbanity

Domitius Marsus [*a famous poet in the time of Augustus*] wrote a very fine treatise on the concept of urbanity. In it, he adds certain well-put sayings to the categories I've enumerated that aren't technically funny, but that do produce a smile through their own special charm and that are suitable for even the gravest occasions. He's

de risu sed de urbanitate est opus institutum,
quam propriam esse nostrae civitatis ait et sērò
sic intellegi coeptam, postquam Urbis appella-
tione, etiam si nomen proprium non adiceretur,
Romam tamen accipi sit receptum. [104] Eam-
que sic finit:

> "Urbanitas" est virtus quaedam in breve
> dictum coacta et apta ad delectandos mov-
> endosque homines in omnem affectum
> animi, maxime idonea ad resistendum vel
> lacessendum, prout quaeque res ac persona
> desiderat.

Cui si brevitatis exceptionem detraxeris, omnīs
orationis virtutes complexa sit. Nam si constat
rebus et personis, quod in utrisque oporteat

right: they *are* "urbane," but they don't inherently produce laughter. [103] He adds them, you see, because his book is not about laughter but "urbanity," which, he says, is a special feature of our society. On his account, the word started being understood in that sense at a late period when, even without adding the proper name, people got used to having the expression "The City" (*Urbs*) mean "Rome."[80] [104] And here's how he defines it:

> "Urbanity" is a sort of power packed into a pithy saying. It is calculated to delight and engage the full gamut of human emotions, and it is especially suited for challenging or fighting back, as the circumstances or person dictate.

And if you leave out pithiness, his definition covers *all* the virtues of oratory, because if it's a question of "circumstances and persons" and

dicere, perfectae eloquentiae est. [105] Cur autem brevem esse eam voluerit, nescio, quom īdem atque in eodem libro dicat fuisse ét in multis narrandi urbanitatem. Paulò post, ita finit, Catonis, ut ait, opinionem secutus:

Urbanus homo erit cuius multa bene dicta responsaque erunt, et qui in sermonibus circulis conviviis, item in contionibus, omni denique loco ridicule commodeque dicet.

[106] Quas si recipimus finitiones, quidquid bene dicetur, ét urbane dicti nomen accipiet. Ceterùm illi qui hoc proposuerat consentanea fuit illa divisio, ut dictorum urbanorum alia "seria," alia "iocosa," alia "media" faceret: nam

what you should say in either instance, then that *is* perfect eloquence. [105] I don't get why he wanted it to be "pithy," though, since he also—and in the very same book—claims that in many authors, there is also an "urbanity of narrative." A bit later, following Cato (as he says), he defines it as follows:

> The urbane person will be one possessed of many clever remarks and replies, and who speaks—in conversation, at social gatherings, at parties, public meetings and, frankly, in *every* circumstance—with appropriate humor.

[106] If we accept these definitions, then any clever remark will also count as an "urbane" remark. Moreover, the brains behind that idea then split "urbane remarks" into subcategories, with some being "serious," others "funny," and others "half-and-half." That made sense, since

est eadem omnium bene dictorum. Verùm mihi etiam "iocosa" quaedam videntur posse in "non satis urbana" referri. [107] Nam meo quidem iudicio, illa est urbanitas, in qua nihil absonum, nihil agreste, nihil inconditum, nihil peregrinum neque sensu neque verbis neque ore gestuve possit deprendi, ut non tám sit in singulis dictis quám in toto colore dicendi, qualis apud Graecos "Atticismŏs" ille, reddens Athenarum proprium saporem.

[108] Ne tamen iudicium Marsi, hominis eruditissimi, subtraham, seria partitur in tria genera, (*1*) "honorificum," (*2*) "contumeliosum," (*3*) "medium."

(*1*) Ét honorifici ponit exemplum, Ciceronis "Pro Q. Ligario" apud Caesarem,

"Qui nihil soles oblivisci—nisi iniurias,"

those are the same subcategories for "clever remarks." Still, it seems to me that even some
jokes can't really count as urbane, [107] since in
my own view, urbanity means that nothing off,
crude, tasteless, or strange can be seized on in
the meaning, language, facial expression, or gestures; and it's not so much a matter of this or
that word as it is the whole tenor of speech,
much the way that in Greek, the concept of "At-
ticism" conjures up the stylish taste of Athens.

[108] Still, so as not to cheat Marsus of his
opinion—he *is* a very impressive man—he di-
vides "serious" into three classes: (*1*) ennobling, (*2*) disparaging, and (*3*) half-and-half.

(*1*) As an example of ennobling, he cites
Cicero's remark before Caesar in his speech
In Defense of Quintus Ligarius:

"You never forget anything, except
injuries."

[109] (2) ét contumeliosi, quod Attico scripsit de
Pompeio et Caesare:

"Habeo quem fugiam; quem sequar non
habeo,"

(3) ét medii, quod "ἀποφθεγματικόν" vocat, ut
est "In Catilinam" quom dixit,

"Neque gravem mortem accidere viro
forti posse, nec immaturam consulari, nec
miseram sapienti."

Quae omnia sunt optime dicta; sed cur proprie
nomen urbanitatis accipiant, non video.

[110] Quod si non totius, ut mihi videtur, orationis color meretur, sed etiam singulis dictis
tribuendum est, illa potius urbana esse dixerim

[109] (2) For disparaging, he cites what Cicero wrote Atticus about Pompey and Caesar:

> "I know which of them to avoid; I don't know which to follow."

(3) And for half-and-half, which he calls "apophthegmatic," he quotes *Against Catiline* [4.3] where Cicero says,

> "Death *cannot* come grievous for a gentleman, nor early for a statesman, nor tragic for a philosopher."

These are all very clever remarks; but as to why they should be particularly called "urbane"— that I don't see.

[110] But if it isn't the tenor of a whole speech that merits the name (as I would say), but it's to be granted to individual remarks, too, I'd then be inclined to call remarks "urbane" that come

quae sunt generis eiusdem ex quo ridicula ducuntur et tamen ridicula non sunt; ut de Pollione
Asinio—seriis iocisque pariter accommodato—
dictum est esse eum

"omnium horarum,"

[111] et de actore facile dicente ex tempore,

"Ingenium eum 'in numerato' habere;"

etiam Pompei, quod refert Marsus, in Ciceronem diffidentem partibus:

"Transi ad Caesarem! Me timebis."

Erat enim, si de re minore aut alio animo aut
denique non ab ipso dictum fuisset, quod

from the same category as jokes, but that aren't actually jokes. An example is the remark about Asinius Pollio, who was equally adept at both serious and comic matters:

"He's a 24-hour-a-day guy."

[111] And of a lawyer who excelled at speaking off the cuff:

"He keeps his cleverness in cash."

There's also Pompey's swipe (which Marsus quotes) at Cicero, when he was chickening out about their alliance:

"Go join Caesar, and you can be afraid of *me!*"

You see, if that remark had been made about something less serious or in a different spirit, or,

posset inter ridicula numerari. [112] Etiam illud quod Cicero Caerelliae scripsit, reddens rationem cur illa C. Caesaris tempora tam patienter toleraret,

"Haec aut animo Catonis ferenda sunt—
aut Ciceronis stomacho."

"Stomachus" enim ille habet aliquid ioco simile.

Haec quae monebam, dissimulanda mihi non fuerunt; in quibus ut erraverim, legentīs tamen non decepi, indicatā ét diversā opinione, quam sequi magis probantibus liberum est.

■ ■ ■

for that matter, not by Pompey himself, then it could have counted as a joke. [112] There's also what Cicero wrote Caerellia to explain why he was putting up with life under Caesar so patiently—

> "To handle this, you need the heart of a Cato or the stomach of a Cicero."

—because there is something inherently funny about the word "stomach."

All these tips I've been giving—I couldn't keep them to myself, and though I may have gotten some wrong, I haven't tricked my readers. I made a point of giving the opposite view, and readers are free to follow it if they prefer.

■ ■ ■

EPILOGUE

The theme of our book is *How to Tell a Joke*, but a parting word on *How to Take a Joke* is in order, too. What can you do if you find yourself the target of public ridicule, especially by a higher-up? Plutarch gives us an example from 43 BCE, the year Cicero held office as Consul. Toward the end of that year, Cicero gave a witty speech defending the incoming Consul, Lucius Licinius Murena, on a charge of electoral bribery. Since Murena was obviously guilty, Cicero decided to ridicule the private beliefs of the opposing counsel, the great Cato the Younger, to distract the jury (see *In Defense of Murena* 61–65). Cato was a devout follower of Stoicism, still a minority denomination of philosophy in

Rome at that time. What happened next? Plutarch liked the anecdote so much he told it twice (*Comparison of Cicero and Demosthenes* 1.5 and *Life of Cato the Younger* 21). As the story goes, says Plutarch,

> When Cato was prosecuting Murena, Cicero—who was Consul at the time—spoke in his defense. And *because* it was Cato, Cicero kept ridiculing Stoics and their silly "paradoxes." When loud laughter spread from the audience to the jury, Cato gave a wry smile and, to those sitting around him, quipped,
>
> > "What a hilarious Consul we have, folks!"

That's it: no rage, no whining, no crying anti-Stoicism, no going lower, no one-upmanship,

but the simple use of inclusive language to frame the jokester as a clown, a buffoon, and regrouping the crowd right back on him. So twirl a finger and roll your eyes if it happens to you. For Plutarch, that strategy trumps 'em all.

NOTES

1. In point of fact, Rome elected *two* Consuls each year, rather than (say) a Consul and a Vice Consul, and they served jointly. (Cicero's co-Consul in 63 BCE was a venal thug named Gaius Antonius Hybrida, son of the Mark Antony in the dialogue that follows.)

2. *Saturnalia* 2.1.10–12. Modern scholars have identified 53 jokes from Tiro's collection (printed in Mueller 1879).

3. *Comparison of Cicero and Demosthenes* 1.4: Κικέρων δὲ πολλαχοῦ τῷ σκωπτικῷ (= *dicacitas*, ridicule) πρὸς τὸ βωμολόχον (= *scurrilitas*, stand-up) ἐκφερόμενος.

4. Ibid., 1.4: πράγματα σπονδῆς ἄξια γέλωτι καὶ παιδιᾷ κατειρωνευόμενος ἐν ταῖς δίκαις εἰς τὸ χρειῶδες ἠφείδει τοῦ πρέποντος.

5. *Satires* 1.10.14–15.

6. 221. Philip Melanchthon, mentioned later, makes the same point (1555, A6v).

7. An inflection point in Roman history, the "Social War" is no laughing matter. It is, however, sometimes jokingly called The War of Dependence, because it saw Rome's "allies" (*socii*) make war on Rome—*not* in order to break free from its empire, but to obtain citizenship in it.

8. Elsewhere: *Brutus* 177 and *On Duties* 1.108 and 1.133; here: 3.30 and 2.98 later.

9. Pigman 2019.

10. Morreall 2016.

11. Sankey 1998, xv, emphasis original.

12. Stein 2020.

13. Saltveit 2020a and Saltveit 2020b.

14. *The Best Kind of Orators* 5.14: *In quibus non verbum pro verbo necesse habui reddere, sed genus omne verborum vimque servavi. Non enim ea me adnumerare lectori putavi oportere, sed tamquam appendere.*

15. Latin: Macrobius's *Saturnalia* 7.3.7; Greek: Plutarch's *Life of Cicero* 26.5.

16. Compare Jay Sankey (1998, xvi): "There aren't a great many books written about stand-up comedy, but those I've seen often have pages and pages of jokes written by famous stand-up comics. Laughing at great jokes by professionals can be fun, but I'm not convinced it really teaches one much about stand-up comedy."

17. Caesar puns on *leve* (lighthearted) and *lēve* (slippery). The word he uses to signal the pun, *quippe*, means, "sure, right." In time, that word took on a sarcastic tone, "sure, riiiight," and eventually turned into our word *quip*.

18. Caesar Strabo's much older half-brother is a man named Catulus, which means "wise" but is identical to the word "puppy." Catulus was Consul in 102 BCE, and has been participating in the dialogue before our extract begins.

19. The real proverb is "pig teaching Minerva." Caesar's variation flatters Crassus as the divine source of wisdom and the arts.

20. Democritus of Abdera (ca. 460–ca. 370 BC), the founder of Greek atomism, was known in antiquity as "the laughing philosopher."

21. Like the Latin Quarter of Paris or New Orleans's French Quarter, Caesar's word *regio* denotes one of the four "quarters" or neighborhoods of the city of Rome (Suburana, Esquilina, Collina, Palatina).

22. Caesar illustrates his point in real time by punning on *saepe* (1) "often" and (2) "an enclosure" (ablative of *saepes*).

23. Referring here to the distinction made in sections 218–222 between "shtick" or stand-up and "sick burns" or street-performance comedy.

24. This is *not* the same distinction Caesar made in section 218, but a new (and major) one.

25. Apparently, he means "clean up" or "get clean" both literally and metaphorically, the latter alluding to his buffoonery or perhaps to ill-gotten gains.

26. This paragraph is apparently the first notice in history of observational comedy ("Did you ever notice . . . ?" "What's the deal with . . . ?").

27. This one's tough. For interpretation, I mostly follow Adkin (2010). The "old expression" is equivalent to "All good? No problems?" but it literally means "Nothing limping, eh?" Glaucia apparently updates the old word with a slangy pronunciation.

28. Literally: He's a real "Calvus" ("Baldy"), alright: he's happy to say practically nothing (i.e., he speaks "baldly," unadorned).

29. The immortal "Funny How?" scene in the 1990 film *Goodfellas* is based on this distinction; see the introduction.

30. Nobody has a clue what this means. If the pun lies in *nucula* (little nut), which is also a name, the translation "kernel" (colonel) should hint at it. Or, if this is the same Decius as in 277 later, it may lie in *confixum* (to pierce or penetrate).

31. That is, "priceless" versus "unsellable." Compare the quip of Moses Hadas (1900–1966): "Thank you for sending me a copy of your book; I'll waste no time reading it."

32. The pun lies in the phrase translated "Not a denarius more!" It can also mean "I have nothing further to say."

33. *Impudicus* is slang for "gay." The Latin pun on *adversus* (facing) and *aversus* (facing away) is equivalent to "top" and "bottom."

34. Rome's Campus Martius was the site of (1) army physical training and (2) elections, for which Cassius evidently distributed bribes. "Youngblood" is my best shot at translating the name of Neoptolemus, the legendary son of Achilles who made his debut fighting in the Trojan War.

35. The *Lex Licinia Mucia*. As Consul, Crassus established it in 95 BCE to investigate claims to citizenship by those whose parents were undocumented.

36. In Roman comedy, from which this quote probably comes, metrosexual sons are always cheat-

ing their fathers out of money to spend on fast living. The implication is that the son used money he was supposed to pass on as a bribe for his own purposes.

37. Like the next example, this one is subtle. "No alarm" means "no, I won't be getting up early on your behalf."

38. The pun is *ex tui animi sententia*, which can mean (1) "Do you solemnly swear . . . ?" and (2) "the way you wanted."

39. A common proverb around the ancient Mediterranean, showing up in the Bible as well as Greek and Roman literature.

40. That is, (1) military company and (2) crowds.

41. In the legendary history of the Trojan War, this Ajax raped Cassandra, the prophetess who was cursed to tell the truth but never be believed. "Oileus" means "the son of King Oileus," but to Roman ears presumably sounded as close to Latin *oleum* (oil) as "oily" does in English, with all the grim connotations that the association implies.

42. The author's grandfather and father respectively.
43. Scipio's co-Censor, Mummius, had supported Burrows; Scipio implies that the gods consequently changed the climate to punish Rome.
44. A free translation of a very knotty piece of Latin.
45. Some think this man is not named Lucullus but Lucilius, the famous satirist.
46. In 133 BCE, an inflection point in Roman history.
47. The Latin pun is on *ferre* (1) to sponsor a law and (2) to offer a bribe.
48. A reference to Cicero's six published speeches attacking Gaius Verres, a corrupt governor of Sicily.
49. "Zaps" (*frangit*) is a brilliant rhetorical ambiguity. *Frangere* means both to weaken or dissipate strong emotions and to literally break something. Quintilian's idea here seems to be that laughter's violent shaking of the body serves to physically shake apart embodied emotions like anger or hatred.

NOTES

50. Urbanity is treated at greater length beginning in section 102.

51. So says the Latin text, though you might expect Quintilian to say the opposite, that anything that's funny should be salty, too. Did he get mixed up himself?

52. Cicero says that in *Orator*, section 90. *Dicacitas*, "verbal aggression," has no one-word equivalent in modern English (in Cicero, section 218, the concrete usage is translated "sick burn").

53. In Cicero's speech *In Defense of Caelius* (69).

54. Gabba was a legendary stand-up comedian in the time of Augustus, while the other three were orators of the following generations. Quintilian quotes some of their greatest hits in the following pages.

55. Quintilian adds a fillip of his own by punning on *condīta* (pepper, add jokes) and *condita* (craft the narrative). He'll do it again in section 96.

56. The Latin pun, on *respicere*, is clearer: to (1) "have some respect for" a mitigating factor, and (2) look around.

57. Arion was a legendary musician of ancient Greece who nearly drowned in the Mediterranean Sea. A dolphin rescued him on its back and carried him to safety.

58. The pun in Latin is on "I too" (*quoque*) and "o cook" (*coque*). As with many other Ciceronian quips quoted later where no citation is given, Quintilian probably took the joke from Tiro's collection (see the introduction).

59. That is, "beholden and unreliable" and literally "whipped" (by his father). The Latin pun is a little different: (1) "flighty" and (2) "whipped."

60. Like *tardus* ("slow" or "too slow"), *sero* can mean either "late" or "too late." The case referred to is covered in Cicero's extant speech *In Defense of Milo*. Cicero makes a similar joke in section 275.

61. That is, as in Orwell's Newspeak.

62. Terence was the Shakespeare of ancient Rome. In his comedy *Phormio*, the title character apparently wore a dusky mask. As for the wit-

ness, bankers' fingertips allegedly got blackened from handling all the coins. My translation alludes to the green eyeshades once associated with bankers.

63. Lentulus and Scipio were both Consuls who looked, respectively, like an actor and an apprentice butcher named Spinther and Serapio (see Valerius Maximus 9.14). (Being an actor in ancient Rome was held in very low regard.)

64. Compare Cicero, section 217.

65. In this section, Quintilian refers to some of the near-infinite technical terms used in Greek and Roman oratory.

66. It's impossible to tell whether the last word is *incidisse* (fell on), *incīdisse* (cut into, incise), or a pun on both, as the translation presupposes.

67. After Fabia left him, this Dolabella (Publius Cornelius Dolabella, died 43 BCE) went on to marry Cicero's daughter, Tullia. (See the volume *How to Grieve* in this series.)

68. The modern analogue would be "Jewish" and "Muslim" (or vice versa).

69. This is wittier in Latin than English, since Latin has hardly any verbal pairs like *ire* (go) and *redire* (go back).

70. Apparently two ambiguities. *Dividere* (split) means (1) to share and (2) to destroy. *Perdes* means (1) you'll lose (your case) and (2) you'll ruin it (the boat).

71. A best guess at a baffling punch line, since no one knows what the key word, *subcenare*, actually means (it appears only here in Latin). It seems likely to mean "start eating before everyone is served," and if so, then Gabba's jest apparently reinterprets it as "eat the bottom of."

72. Sparrows are highly social, randy birds that eat bread and water. Romans kept them as house pets.

73. Sarcastic and ambiguous: (1) "I believe it as if it were true," and (2) "You've cherished my family as little as you cherish the truth."

74. An epic demonstration of the thing in action. As in section 39, *conditur* can mean "composed, built up on" or (pronounced *condītur*) "pep-

pered, built up" with jokes. His ambiguity reads as a response to Caesar's pun on *leve* in Cicero, section 218.

75. Odysseus, himself a "crafty and complicated man," was often called "son of Laertes" (Laertius). In this quotation (from an unknown tragedy), Cicero changes "Laertius" to "Lartius."

76. This is one of Cicero's jokes that Plutarch translated (*Life of Cicero* 7.6); his punch line is almost verbatim: "καὶ μὴν ἐπὶ τῆς οἰκίας (ἔφη) τὴν Σφίγγα ἔχεις." ("And yet, you have the Sphinx at home.")

77. That is, "How can he have a yard sale? He has nothing left to sell."

78. Alternatively, the punch line could mean "The side would've been better" (i.e., a mortal wound).

79. Evidently meaning sections [28] to [35] or [57]: it is hard to tell which, because Quintilian seems to have gone on adding in examples after completing the theoretical outline of his treatise. (Many years later, Freud would do the

same thing in successive editions of his own treatise on *Jokes and Their Relation to the Unconscious*.)

80. In other words, like "human" and "humane," "urban" and "urbane" were originally the same word. The moral quality of the second word emerged from the first.

BIBLIOGRAPHY
AND FURTHER READING

Fantham 2004 is the best introduction to the historical background and characters in Cicero's treatise, Corbeill 1996 the best analysis of its political context, and Beard 2014 the best overview of the comedic contexts of both treatises. For everything else, Leeman, Pinkster, and Rabbie 1989 is a goldmine: humor, philosophy, rhetoric, the rest. Those who cannot read German will appreciate the notes in May and Wisse 2001, which helpfully distill many of the most salient points.

Adkin, Neil. 2010. "A 'Limp' Joke? Cicero, 'De Oratore' II, 249," *Latomus* 69: 706–708.

Beard, Mary. 2014. *Laughter in Ancient Rome: On Joking, Tickling, and Cracking Up*. Oakland: University of California Press.

Bowen, Barbara C. 2003. "A Neglected Renaissance Art of Joking." *Rhetorica* 21, no. 3: 137–148.

Corbeill, Anthony. 1996. *Controlling Laughter: Political Humor in the Late Roman Republic.* Princeton, NJ: Princeton University Press.

Delius, Matthew (Matthaeus). 1555. *De Arte Iocandi libri quattuor.* Wittenberg: Kreutzer, Veit. VD16 D 451 (= *Verzeichnis der im deutschen Sprachbereich erschienenen Drucke des XVI. Jahrhunderts,* Stuttgart: Hiersemann, 1983–).

Fantham, Elaine. 2004. *The Roman World of Cicero's* De Oratore. Oxford: Oxford University Press.

Kumaniecki, Kazimierz (ed.). 1969. *M. Tulli Ciceronis Scripta quae manserunt omnia*, fasc. 3: *De oratore.* Leipzig: Teubner.

Leeman, Anton D., Harm Pinkster, and Edwin Rabbie (eds.). 1989. *De Oratore libri III*, vol. 3 (2.99–290). Heidelberg: Winter.

May, James M., and Jakob Wisse (tr.). 2001. *Cicero: On the Ideal Orator (De oratore).* Oxford: Oxford University Press.

Melanchthon, Philip. 1555 (April 17). "A Few Thoughts on the Art of Joking" (*Pauca de materia huius operis*). Embedded in Delius 1555, A31–8v. (Summarized in Bowen 2003, 141–142.)

Morreall, John. 2016. "Philosophy of Humor." In *The Stanford Encyclopedia of Philosophy*, ed. Edward N. Zalta. Available at https://plato.stanford.edu/archives/win2016/entries/humor/ (accessed June 11, 2020).

Mueller, Carl Friderich Wilhelm (ed.). 1879. "Ciceronis Facete Dicta." In *M. Tullii Ciceronis Scripta quae manserunt omnia*, vol. 4.3, pp. 341–350. Leipzig: Teubner.

Pigman, G. W. (ed.). 2019. *Giovanni Gioviano Pontano: The Virtues and Vices of Speech.* Cambridge, MA: Harvard University Press.

Russell, Donald A. (ed.). 2001. *Quintilian: The Orator's Education*, vol. 3 (books 6–8). Cambridge, MA: Harvard University Press.

Saltveit, Mark. 2020a. "Comedians as Daoist Missionaries." *Journal of Daoist Studies* 13: 213–221.

———. 2020b. Personal interview of April 8.

Sankey, Jay. 1998. *Zen and the Art of Stand-Up Comedy*. London: Routledge.

Stein, Joel. 2020. Personal interview of March 19.